TRUE
FAITH

**The believer's journey from
self-reliance to God-reliance**

Wouter van der Westhuizen

First Published 2025 by Wouter van der Westhuizen
Copyright © 2025 Wouter van der Westhuizen

ISBN 978-1-0672379-4-3 (Print)
ISBN 978-1-0672379-3-6 (eBook)

Cover and interior crafted with love by the team at
www.myebook.online

MYEBOOK
WE EMPOWER AUTHORS

Contents

Why this title?

You may ask what the purpose of the first word in the title is. The word "true" depicts an objective description and I feel this is necessary because of the many ways that faith is being taught, misused, distorted, misunderstood and miscommunicated. As a result of the subjective way that faith is often used by believers, its true essence has become person-centric.

As the overall purpose of Scripture is to glorify God, it should be expected that everything contained in Scripture and taught from Scripture should follow the same purpose. Faith, as taught in Scripture, should always glorify God. Originating as a gift from God, faith should not be repurposed as a human endeavour to glorify man's achievements and gratify human desires.

Faith as a gift from God will always remain true and pure. People are at fault when God's gift is taught and applied inappropriately. Faith is not a human success story, nor is it a tribute to the human spirit. Faith is not meant to elevate man's ego, but to humble the flesh as it expresses its need for God's provision in all things.

When this happens, faith serves to bring glory to God. Romans 1:17 says that those who are justified, or saved, will live and walk by faith.

> For in the gospel the righteousness of God is revealed—a righteousness that is by faith from first to last, just as it is written: "The righteous will live by faith." (NIV)

Faith is the mechanism through which a person is born again and how they are to live their Christian lives. Imagine the problems and frustrations believers will experience in this life and the life to come if they misunderstand what faith truly is?

True faith is a spiritual force and should be exercised in the spirit to affect the natural world. Faith is not meant to be misused as a tool to gain what God has not permitted. We often see how believers employ faith like a circus animal, trained to perform tricks to gain profits for its owners. This is how many believers are influenced by televangelists who flaunt their wealth and promote their success stories and faith formulas for others to emulate. The use of faith in this way does not glorify God.

In this book we deal with a powerful form of religion – the power of "believing in myself". This is not about self-confidence; it refers to a person's belief in themselves rather than in God. This is a destructive ideology and has been widespread in the world since the days of Adam. It is the oldest parareligion on earth and, deservingly, it receives the harshest punishment in God's Word. It is not true faith.

This book communicates true faith as a gift to empower people to receive from God what they cannot achieve in their own will, wisdom, strength and ability.

Trust in the Lord with all your heart, And lean not on your own understanding; In all your ways acknowledge Him, And He shall direct your paths. Proverbs 3: 5,6 (NKJV)

The author of Proverbs clearly distinguishes between God's provision and a person's ability to live independently from God. He does not deny humankind's abilities, but suggests we are to submit all our ways to God, which is the prerequisite to receiving from God what we need.

Now faith is the substance of things hoped for, the evidence of things not seen. Hebrews 11:1 (NKJV)

Reading Hebrews 11:1 and not referencing Proverbs 3:5-6 can cause the believer to either misunderstand faith or fail to properly apply it in their Christian lives. This book sets out to explain how the aspects of faith mentioned in Proverbs 3, Hebrews 11 and other Scriptures play a key role in developing our faith, also known as our "trust" in God.

This book will look at what Paul says in Romans 1:17 about the Gospel and how it's possible for people to reach out and communicate with someone they cannot see. We will look at how people can achieve a righteous position before God, allowing them to petition God for their immediate daily needs. We will examine why so many Christians have not been able to live the way God wants them to. We investigate the common misconception that faith is largely a "get what I want" tool.

We will explore Paul's statement that the Gospel, which is received by faith alone, anchors people's hopes, unlike the false hope they have in their own abilities. Faith is trust in God. It requires the total surrender of a person's abilities and dreams and brings them to a ground zero – where there's no boasting in the flesh (Ephesians 2:8-9).

Faith as expressed in the Bible, when read in isolation, can be distorted and morph into a means of selfish gains without having to live a pure life. The distortion is because it focuses on a person's fleshly desires and does not glorify God. The so-called "faith movement" has largely taught faith as a stand-alone mechanism to enrich yourself and to create your own comfort zones. But faith or trust in God only functions inside the confines of a relationship. As soon as sin sets in, the trust in the relationship is violated.

My desire for this book is to allow every believer to fulfil what Paul said; that their lives will be lived by faith so that God will be glorified. The idea is not to present a theoretical book on faith, but to explain some of the practical steps the believer needs to understand when walking by faith. I also address what to do when God's answer is delayed.

I trust that some of the unknowns and unexpected aspects related to faith will be laid bare to the believer.

Chapter 1

The cost of not knowing faith

While writing this book, I experienced a situation that compelled me further in my efforts. It was so in line with the theme that I just had to include it at the beginning to assist the reader to understand the heart of the book. The words, "Did you not know?" will ring in the heart of every believer who reads this book.

I own a small modern car and decided to save some money and replace the brake pads myself when the indicator light warned me that the disc pads needed replacing, but it didn't say whether it was the front or rear pads that needed replacing. So I set off to the dealership to buy both sets. I was shocked when the salesperson gave me the bill. I swallowed twice and after asking if there was not a mistake, I swiped my credit card to pay for the most expensive brake pads I had ever bought.

Once home, I made light work of the front brake pads. It was when I got to the rear brake pads that something went drastically wrong. After taking off the pads I heard an alarm sounding in the car. I had forgotten to disengage the auto handbrake, which caused the brake calliper to be damaged. Yes, I had Googled to see what to do, but the videos I watched made no mention of any auto-park brake function. I had to have a tow truck deliver my broken car to the dealership. I arrived with the tow truck and sat down at the service adviser's desk to be briefed regarding the costs of repairing my car. While working on the quote, the dealership assistant gave me a strange look. She said: 'Can I ask you a straight question?' She looked over her reading glasses and said: 'I am puzzled. Why did you do this? Did you not know your car came with a full factory maintenance plan that covers everything on the car for the next five years.' I was speechless when I heard that not only the expensive battery I had recently replaced, as well as the expensive front and rear brake pads I installed were all covered by the maintenance plan. She kept repeating the question: 'Did you not know? Were you not aware that everything you did was covered by the maintenance plan?'

I have done brake-pad replacements on many cars and I was sure I could handle it. I felt secure in my abilities to do the replacements. I believed in myself. The woman's questions started ringing another bell in my mind while I sat at her desk. For the average believer who fights their way through the many challenges they face daily, faith is a "cannot do without" necessity. Never mind these challenges, they also often have the enemy pursuing them and God allowing difficulties in order to develop the believer's faith. It's not an easy road to walk when the believer has many obstacles and opposition to overcome while being ignorant about the inner workings of faith.

God never meant for the believer to be born again in their own strength, nor to face life in this broken world on their own.

What Paul says in Romans 1:17 rings loudly. We've been given the spiritual gift of faith to empower, equip and assist the believer to walk by faith. It's a spiritual force that allows the believer to live a natural life on earth using supernatural power. Not only does this power save and cause rebirth to happen but it also empowers believers to walk in this broken world as victors over the enemy and circumstances. To apply faith appropriately, the believer needs to be informed. An uninformed believer will act in a similar way to me when attempting to service my own car. I possessed the complete maintenance plan yet I went to great lengths to use my own misinformation to incorrectly install the brake pads in a complex system. I was the one who suffered.

All we need for a Godly life

For many believers, faith works in the same way. Apostle Peter says through our knowledge of Jesus and His divine power, we have received all we need for a Godly life (2 Peter 1:3).

By deciding to become informed and by knowing what is contained in God's Word, we can inform, equip and empower ourselves. My experiences and knowledge that I had gained in the past when servicing cars was of no use when I tackled the challenge of servicing a modern car.

Equally so, by understanding faith and knowing how its workings are described in Scripture, the believer can begin to access everything God has included in the salvation package that He has freely given us in Christ Jesus. The service adviser said to me: 'Whenever your car needs anything, contact me and we will do it for you. No one should struggle to have their car properly serviced.' Every believer should be able to go to God's Word and through prayer, ask God when they need assistance. No believer should battle through life in their own power and wisdom.

The words "Did you not know?" were not pleasant to hear. But what followed when the service advisor gave me my account for the repairs was the most painful. She said: 'This whole mess could have been prevented if only you had read the conditions in your motor maintenance and service plan. This is going to be your most expensive mistake ever.' Imagine that this is what God will say to believers who didn't bother to become informed while walking on earth. Knowing how faith, which is God's gift to every believer on earth, could have changed their life on earth and could have secured a great eternal reward.

> And without faith it is impossible to please God, because anyone who comes to him must believe that he exists and that he rewards those who earnestly seek him. Hebrews 11:6 (NIV).

The costly realisation for the ignorant believer is that all the hard work, their reliance on self and missed opportunities happened because they didn't know that God had already made everything they needed available to them for free. People's greatest asset is also their greatest stumbling block. Their stubborn insistence to believe in themselves and rely on themselves prevents faith from functioning in their lives. The serpent targeted Adam and Eve's trust in God and he does the same to every other believer.

Chapter 2

What true faith is

To properly understand what Paul meant in Romans 1:17 by, 'The just shall live by faith,' we need to go back to where the people of God began living by faith. Although the term "faith" is not often used in the Old Testament, the term "trust" is most commonly used. In the New Testament, Jesus uses faith and trust interchangeably (John 14:1).

At the start of this book, I want to establish a key theme from Scripture. Israel underwent three major steps in their existence. These three steps are also visible in the life of every believer. In the Old Testament Israel's time, we see their exodus from Egypt (their freedom from Egyptian slavery), their journey through the Wilderness (testing, development and purification) and then their inhabiting of the Promised Land (inheritance, peace and fulfilment).

This same theme is found in the New Testament regarding salvation. The believer is justified by faith (freedom from sin slavery), then follows sanctification (washing by God's Word and testing)

5

and finally glorification (eternal inheritance and peace, present with God in the heavenly city). Please note that both the Old and New Testament themes are journeys taken by faith alone. Without God, the journeys would not have been possible.

The book of Hebrews warns us not to make the same mistake that the Israelites made. They didn't put their faith in God and suffered greatly for it. Interestingly, not trusting God is described as sin in Hebrews 3:12, 19. By faith, some of the people of Israel went from Egyptian slavery through the Wilderness and inherited the Promised Land. Many did not make it to the Promised Land because of their unbelief (Hebrews 4:2).

The Old Testament tells us about Israel's major transformation from living in Egypt to their journey through the Wilderness. In Egypt, everything was handed to them on a plate. Although they were slaves, everything was supplied by the Egyptians. After leaving Egypt, the almost two million people of Israel became hungry in the desert and their first complaint was that they remembered the food and wanted to return to Egyptian captivity (Numbers 11:1-5).

God planned Israel's Wilderness walk with the purpose of undoing the reliance they had developed on what they had in Egypt. The first of the Ten Commandments stipulates exactly what God wanted to replace their reliance on Egypt with. He wanted to be their source of life, protection and provision. The Egyptians were polytheists, but the message God gave to Israel was the opposite:

Hear, O Israel: The Lord our God, the Lord is one.
Deuteronomy 6:4 (NIV)

The Lord God of Israel's first command to His people was that He is their only God and that they were to serve no other god but the Lord God.

The first two Commandments given at Mount Sinai eliminated Israel's dependence on any other god. God was their only God and they had to learn to depend on Him and Him alone. He was to be their source for everything they needed. As their journey started, we see that within the first few weeks, the people of God ran out of water and food. God delivered to them what they needed and in doing so, He demonstrated that they had to learn to trust Him for all they needed. God knew what they needed before they asked Him. The Wilderness journey was a method God used to empty the Israelites out of their dependence on themselves, their possessions and the Egyptian way of life. God was in the process of creating in the Israelites a new way of living – a new culture of trusting Him daily for all they needed.

Today, we are to undergo the same change after we are saved. We need to be emptied of our reliance on ourselves, the world and our own wisdom. After all, faith is a God-given tool we are to employ to achieve what is impossible to man.

Connecting faith and the Word of God

We need to re-establish and confirm our understanding and conviction that the Word of God expresses who God is. It speaks on His behalf. Hebrews says that Jesus, the Word of God, is an exact representation of the Father's nature (Hebrews 1:3).

The words Jesus spoke are alive, they're true, they're eternal, inerrant and spiritual in nature. When God spoke creation into being in Genesis 1, the spiritual gave rise to the natural. It's important to understand that the spiritual has authority over the natural. In Genesis, God's Word shaped what we see as the natural world around us and His Word will still shape or alter the natural realm around us. When we act on God's Word, we unleash the same spiritual power that is seen in Genesis 1 to act on our behalf.

The Spirit gave rise to the Word of God. In the Trinity, the Father speaks the Word and the Spirit is the power within the Word. Romans 10:17 says that faith comes through the Word of God. Faith, being a spiritual gift, empowers us to trust the Word of God when we hear or read it. Let's briefly visit the other options available to us.

The opposite of God's Word includes secular teachings such as worldly ideologies, false religions that prescribe steps to inner purity, regulations that have an appearance of wisdom with self-imposed worship, false humility and their harsh treatment of the body (Colossians 2:23), and ancestral beliefs, instructions, and teachings and doctrines of demons (1 Timothy 4:1). None of these teachings are divinely inspired, and note that some, if not all, are teachings from the enemy though demonic inspiration. There's no truth apart from God's Word. Faith can only work if underpinned by the Word of God. There is no other body of truth that is inerrant, unchangeable, eternal, alive and divinely authoritative in which people can place their hope. No other body of beliefs can claim that when spoken or quoted, it can bring forth life as the Word of God did in Genesis 1.

True faith, which expresses deep trust, must always be linked to a reliable, trustworthy and accurate body of truth – and the only one is the Word of God. All other bodies of teachings and instruction are manmade, inspired and centred. For people to walk in a way that will ensure their eternal life, they must reach out to someone greater than themselves, more powerful than themselves, and most importantly, someone untainted by sin. The One such person is the Trinity.

Faith defined

> Now faith is the substance of things hoped for, the
> evidence of things not seen. Hebrews 11.1 (**NKJV**)

What is the substance referred to in Hebrews 11:1? The NIV describes faith as 'confidence in what we hope for and assurance about what we do not see'. It comes back to trust that is based on a relationship and not on an ethereal grasping at straws.

Faith is the spiritual gift that helps us build a bridge between this sinful world and a holy God. Faith enables us to walk and see in the Spirit. Faith is God stretching out a helping hand to a person drowning – it is God's gift of faith. Without this gift the unbeliever is unable to put their trust in God to be saved. Before the unbeliever receives what we call "saving faith", they're still in a rebellious state against God. Saving faith enters the heart of the unbeliever to enable them to respond to the call of God and be saved. This gift of faith in the person's heart empowers them to put their faith in Jesus, as stated in John 3:16.

How are faith or trust in God, the work of the Holy Spirit and the Word of God intertwined? How do we receive faith and how is the faith we receive connected to Scripture?

In John 14:1, Jesus tells His disciples that they must not let their hearts be troubled – this is in the face of all the hardships they are about to face. They're scared and He is about to depart. They will soon face the full might of the Roman Empire and the Jewish religious stronghold who planned Jesus' crucifixion. Jesus comforts His disciples as He prepares them for His imminent departure and their need to take over His ministry. They were to go into Jerusalem, then Judea, then Samaria and to the ends of the earth (Acts 1:8).

In John 14:1, Jesus told them they must trust in Him as they had trusted in the Father up to that point. Their ancestors had trusted God since the days of Abraham.

Then in verse 18, Jesus makes it clear that He will not leave them as orphans. He promises He will send them the Holy Spirit (verses 15-17) who will be their advocate and who will remain in them forever.

> And I will ask the Father, and he will give you another
> advocate to help you and be with you forever—the Spirit
> of truth. The world cannot accept him, because it neither
> sees him nor knows him. But you know him, for he lives
> with you and will be in you. John 14: 15-17 (NIV)

Jesus calls the Holy Spirit, the Spirit of truth – an amazing designation for the other person of the Trinity. The purest form of reality is truth, which is always factual, inerrant, unchanging and trustworthy.

When a parent gives a young child a puppy, the gift comes with a set of guidelines to ensure that the child understands the responsibilities of owning a pet. Without the guidelines, the child could neglect the puppy or it could get hurt. It's the parent's responsibility to ensure that the guidelines are always observed and that the child learns about responsibility, compassion, care and love.

Similarly, faith is a gift from the Spirit of God. He gives the believer a gift to help them develop in God's will and His ways. This gift comes with guidelines found in the Word of God. If these guidelines are not followed properly, the gift of faith could morph into a dangerous "tool" in the hands of a believer and it could harm them.

The Word of God provides guidelines on how faith works and how to develop it in the life of the believer. It also teaches the believer the purpose of faith and how to respect the giver of the gift. God is not like an irresponsible parent who gives His children a gift without the necessary training and guidelines to look after the gift. Part of the Spirit's work in our heart is to guide us when reading God's Word. He makes us hungry to know God better and He reveals to us what we read (Ephesians 1:17). He illuminates our understanding through Scripture to know God, His person, His will and His ways. The gift of faith is the "bridge" God builds for us to be introduced to Him and to receive what we need to develop into mature spiritual believers.

Faith is therefore not a stand-alone gift or principle. It is a spiritual gift that requires us to follow the accompanying guidelines so that we always respect the giver, the gift and its principles. Faith must never be handled without the Word of God.

The object of our faith

There is a goal that God is working towards in His eternal plan of salvation. Revelation spells this out when it speaks of the wars to take place, the defeat of the enemy and then the finale, where God dwells with the saints forever. Faith plays a key part in the transformation of the believer, a righteousness from beginning to end (Romans 1:17).

First, it secures the believer's justification (Romans 5:1; Ephesians 2:8,9).

Second, it progressively washes the believer to become more like Jesus in character, actions and nature (2 Corinthians 3:18), which is a lifelong process called sanctification.

Third, it develops a trust in the believer about their death and translation into heaven. It guarantees that when a believer departs from their earthly body, they will immediately be present with God, as Paul says in 2 Corinthians 5:8. Hebrews explains it as the believer looking for another dwelling place better than this earth (Hebrews 13:14).

In Romans, Paul explains, right at the start of this amazing book, that faith has a goal. What he says in Romans 1:5 closes the door to any misapplication of the gift of faith. Many preachers skip this verse and use faith to fulfil their own fleshly desires. Faith has a goal – to bring glory to God. By way of explanation, consider when you sit down to a set menu in a restaurant. The menu is given to you and the waiters bring out the sequence of dishes, which the guests participate in, from start to finish. It would be disrespectful for a guest to refuse a dish or express their desire for one dish over the other. They're there to enjoy what the chef has prepared. The entire meal is a package deal, prepared and served with skill and it's designed to honour the chef. In the same way, faith is like one dish in a set menu God has prepared for us. It cannot be isolated and enjoyed on its own. It forms part of a sequence of steps that embody God's entire plan of salvation for every believer. The goal of faith is to glorify God, and in doing so, faith takes us on a journey.

Faith must run its course from beginning to end to develop the nature of Christ within the believer. It works within the believer from the moment of the sinner's justification (Romans 5:1) until they are eternally present with God. It's therefore clear that faith has a "shelf-life" and becomes obsolete when the believer reaches the state of perfection – being present with God (2 Corinthians 5:8; 1 Corinthians 13:13).

Faith must complete its work of affecting Christlike change within the believer. The work of faith encompasses the spiritual disciplines such as the fruit of the Spirit (Galatians 5:22-23) and patience (James 1:4). Faith plays a crucial role in the transformation of person from an unbeliever to a mature believer, which Paul describes as running the race of faithfulness (1 Corinthians 9:25,26; Philippians 3:12-14; 1 Timothy 6:12). Hebrews 12: 1-3 tells us that Jesus is our focus in all matters of faith. From justification to sanctification to glorification, He is the goal of our faith. His birth, life and salvation work are our pattern for living on earth. Like Jesus, we look forward to our heavenly home (Hebrews 13:14).

We gain insight into the obedience that comes from faith by understanding the patterns God reveals to us in the Old Testament and His dealings with Israel. The whole journey Israel underwent from being freed from Egyptian slavery to their journey through the Wilderness and their eventual habitation of the Promised Land was a process that depended on their trust in God (Hebrews 4:2).

God freed Israel from Egyptian slavery by His mighty hand. This was a process that was based in grace and them trusting God for the blood of the lamb to protect them (Exodus 12:7). Marching free from slavery, God then instructed them to camp at the foot of Mount Sinai so He could address them and give them His decrees and laws (Exodus 20:1-17). Their obedience to these commands would decide the success of every Israelite's journey to the Promised Land. Trusting God was the key aspect God expected of Israel. Scripture details how Israel failed to trust God and how God responded to this failure (Deuteronomy 1:32). It's clear from these patterns that God graciously gives us the gift of faith and expects us to reciprocate His gift by giving Him our undivided devotion and loyalty by obeying His commands. When we read Romans 1:5, we see that Paul is encouraging believers to receive the gift of faith from God and to walk obediently in His commands. Faith must lead the believer towards obedience – and it's important that we understand what this obedience entails.

The objective of our faith is to be like Jesus Christ through a step-by-step transformation (1 Corinthians 11:1). The result, as John says, is to be found in His likeness (1 John 3:2). This means that the believer must undergo a complete transformation from sinner to saint.

> … fixing our eyes on Jesus, the pioneer and perfecter of faith. For the joy set before him he endured the cross, scorning its shame, and sat down at the right hand of the throne of God. Hebrews 12: 2 (NIV)

When you fix your eyes on someone or something, it means you won't be distracted by other options. Just as a husband devotes his love to his wife, so we devote our love to Christ. This devotion to Jesus Christ is what Paul explains in Romans 1:5. He says faith leads to obedience; he's telling us that we're to develop a habit of obeying Jesus just as Jesus obeyed His Father.

A habit is something we form through repeated action, whether good or bad. Romans 1:5 hints at an attitude we need to develop that chooses to obey rather than sin. Because of the innate sinful disposition we are born with, obedience does not come naturally to a believer, which means we must cultivate it as a habit over time. Jesus was born into this world and also had to develop an attitude of obedience to both His natural father and Spiritual Father (Hebrews 5:8). Paul explains this obedience in more detail in Philippians 2:8-10. He says our obedience must be like Jesus' who obeyed His Father even unto death. Jesus died on the cross; our part is the crucifixion of our flesh – the end of our sinful human nature. Our obedience is a sign of our utter devotion and loyalty to God.

If we follow what Paul says about the obedience that comes from our faith, we will fulfil the words of Jesus in John 14:15: 'If you love me, keep my commands.' Jesus says that His Father measures our appreciation of the gift of life He has made available to us, received by faith, by our habitual obedience to what He says. Our walking in step with the commands contained in His Word glorifies the Father and is a testimony to the world. His Word to us came in the form of Jesus who walked the earth. Everything Jesus did, said and abstained from are what we are to emulate – just as Paul encouraged us to do.

Hebrews 1:3 says Jesus is the exact representation of the Father and John 14:9 says: 'Anyone who has seen me has seen the Father.' Jesus accurately explains the Father to us and helps us to interpret who He is – His nature, His will and His ways. For example, when John relates Jesus' cleaning of the temple, John didn't said that Jesus apologised to His Father for what He had done (John 2:13-22). This means that what Jesus did was an exact representation of what the Father's own actions would have been.

When the Father sent Jesus, His intentions were clear. He was sending the exact representation of Himself to us (Hebrews 1:3).

The Person the Father sent would lead us in all He wanted us to know about Himself. Jesus would reveal the Father's expectations for those He created. He also sent the plan detailing how we could live our lives daily to stay obedient to His will and ways. Jesus, the Father's perfect representation, would set the perfect example. He would speak every word and do every deed the Father decided were necessary for us to hear and see (John 12:49). Not only is Jesus the exact image, the representation and an ambassador of the Father, He is also the only way to the Father (John 14:6). Furthermore, Jesus says His words are those of the Father's and they are truth (John 6:63; John 17:17).

We can see from this that it's not logical to put your trust in anything apart from God's Word, or to emulate any other person's life and example. God's message to us, from Genesis to Revelation, is Jesus. It begins and ends with Him. His example is what we should emulate; He's the One we should study and follow. Jesus is God's standard for every believer – He initiates faith in us and by His Word and the Spirit of God, our faith is complete. The end goal of faith that has been given to us by the Father is to transform us into His likeness.

Chapter 3

The grounds for walking by faith

Hebrews 11:1 says faith is defined as an assurance (the substance) of what we hope for and the evidence of what we do not see.

What is this assurance? Hebrews speaks of God being the substance (Hebrews 6:13-20). In this passage and in Hebrews 11 we see how God both made and fulfilled His promises.

What is the evidence? Historical facts are the proof that God promised and fulfilled His Word. The covenant God made with Abraham (Genesis 15) was fulfilled (Hebrews 11:12). The promise of a Saviour (Genesis 3:15) was fulfilled in Jesus' death and resurrection.

The evidence I can rely on is what God did for those mentioned in the Bible; these are irrefutable facts I can place my hope in. This is where I start my walk. By using these examples of God's faithfulness, I gather my own evidence of what God has done for me personally. My hope began with the historical evidence I see in Scripture and it becomes the evidence I see in my own life, which is very powerful. Once I have personally tasted that the Lord is good, no person, no set of circumstances nor challenges will convince me otherwise.

When regarding Jesus as the object of our faith, we must also consider that He's the pure and true Word of the eternal God. His Word is holy; it contains power, it is inerrant and it is nothing but God Himself. It's reliable because God, being of such a pure nature, cannot lie. The Word of God not only contains His will and His ways but it's also an instruction manual on holy living for all of humanity. Romans 10:17 says faith is applied to the hearer through the Word of God. Scripture mentions nothing else – not human effort nor human wisdom, not philosophies nor science. Equally, when we as believers stand on God's Word and apply our faith, we place our trust in His promises.

We need to be careful not to add elements such as our emotions, mind-over-matter, the principles of this world, social patterns and so forth to our faith. Our faith must not be watered down by adding human effort and then, through that, claiming that God must answer our request.

Faith on a deeper level

The word "trust" means to have a firm belief in the reliability or ability of something or someone, although many people use the word in a flippant way. During a testing time of trusting God for a breakthrough, I had to endure a kind of victory-defeat, high-and-low situation several times. I would feel a breakthrough was imminent one day only to face defeat yet again. It felt as if life was draining out of me every time I stood up and was knocked down again.

I was washing dishes in the kitchen when I felt the need to say: 'Lord, I give this problem to you again.' I envisioned myself handing my problem to God and asking Him to intervene. I did again what I had done previously. I gave my problem to God unconditionally with no reserve – I handed it over and fully accepted whatever His decision might be. I continued washing the dishes with a relieved feeling. Suddenly I felt as if the Lord said to me: 'It is easy to say, "Lord take my problem," but it is not so easy to say it to my face.' What immediately transpired was testing of my trust in God. Would I look into His eyes and say I trust Him yet have reservations about the outcome?

This was a deeper level of faith than I had ever experienced before. It purified my trust in God to a point where it must have been a bit similar to what Jesus went through. Having all of heaven at His disposal, Jesus humbled Himself to obey His Father's command. Hanging on the cross, nailed to the wood, there was no way out for Him but to surrender His will and position to facilitate the plan of salvation His Father desired for a sinful world.

In a wedding ceremony, two people are face-to-face when they express their love and commitment to each other, signifying the beginning of a deep trust between them. This face-to-face meeting and the subsequent vows and covenant are a sign of something the Apostle Paul referred to as a 'profound mystery' (Ephesians 5:31-33). Trusting someone goes far beyond expressing a few words; it means always living up to your promises no matter what.

In Scripture, we see Jesus expressing a deep level of trust on several occasions when He spoke to His Father, for instance in John 17 and when He restored Peter in John 21:15-17. Let's look at this account between Jesus and Peter to highlight the deep trust Jesus showed Peter, even in the face of Peter denying Jesus publicly. Jesus did not brush over what Peter had done; He was embarking on a powerful restorative process in Peter's life. Of all people, Peter should have been the last person to lead the believers after what he had done. Yet, what Jesus did was remarkable. He appeared to Peter and the rest of the disciples, ate with them, and then began restoring Peter.

Jesus knew that Peter needed to see that He trusted him. Peter needed to look Jesus in the eyes and hear from Him that he was forgiven. The result of Jesus restoring Peter is seen in the life and words of Peter until his death. I can imagine how difficult it was for Peter when Jesus looked him in the eyes and asked him: 'Simon, son of John, do you love me more than these?' Jesus did this three times. The words Jesus spoke to Peter must have cut incredibly deep; here was Jesus, the Son of God, asking Peter if he loves Him – after Peter had denied him three times. What Peter saw and felt transformed him into one of the most influential leaders in the New Testament. This was similar to the personal encounter Jesus had with Saul, the persecutor of the church (Acts 9:4-8). After that, Saul became Paul and his trust in Jesus was an unbreakable and eternal bond that carried him through the toughest challenges.

A relationship can only deepen to this level after deep trust has been established – as seen in the relationships Jesus had with Peter and Paul. It is not surprising that Jesus entrusted great power to these two men. The deeper the trust, the greater the weight of the call on the person. To understand how important trust is to God, let's look at the fact that God the Father could not entrust any human being with His plan of salvation (John 2:23-25). He had to send His Son to carry the weight of all of humanity's sin, making redemption available to everyone who receives His gift of eternal life.

The greatest asset

Have you ever asked yourself what the most precious commodity known to humanity is? What is the most sought-after resource in the world? What is the most powerful relationship that exists? What is the most reliable connection to have? What is the most trustworthy body of evidence? What is the most profitable asset to invest in? These questions all raise the same point. We as human beings are all looking for something beyond this earth – something we can trust in the midst of a storm.

I recently stood next to a hospital bed where my brother-in-law, John, who had lived a God-honouring life, was dying from heart failure. Hour after hour the alarms rang out every time his blood pressure plummeted and his heart fibrillated. He was losing the battle to stay alive and we, together with the medical team, were unable to make him well. What stood between him and eternal life was one thing – his trust in God. That was all he had to depend on when he finally closed his eyes a few days later. When he breathed his last and went on to be with God, no qualification, no big bank balance, no shareholding and no profitable investment would qualify him to enter heaven. He had no claim to any fame or evidence of good works to hold up as a reason to receive eternal life.

All John had was the trust he had placed in God his whole life. Trust is an asset that takes many years to establish and develop. It outweighs anything else and it's directly connected to God's Son Jesus Christ. Trust is not a thumb-suck, a psychological ideology or an emotional feeling; trust is a relationship with a person you have grown to know intimately.

When John stepped out of his natural body into the spiritual realm to be with God, no power on earth and no human achievement were enough to translate him into the presence of God. Equally, no power on earth could keep him from stepping into the presence of God. What he experienced at the moment his heart stopped, was a sense of falling backwards with his eyes closed into the arms of Jesus. John had let go and let Jesus catch him. This is not a blind faith where "let go and let's see" applies. No, John had spent years developing his faith in God. He began trusting God for the small things, then bigger things and eventually the greatest of all – his eternal life. John followed Jesus' example when hanging on the cross and breathing His last, He said: 'Father, into Your hands I commit my spirit' (Luke 23:46). Jesus placed all His trust in His Father.

There is no other bridge strong enough between this world and the world to come and no more valuable commodity than developing your trust in God. His Word details so many instances where God promised and delivered. When my brother-in-law was unable to reach out to anyone and unable to make himself better, all he had was what he had invested over many years. He cashed in on the promise of eternal life God had given in His Word (John 3:16). John also set an excellent example for his children to follow and his legacy speaks beyond the grave just as Jesus' does.

If heaven is a beautiful garden, then trust is the key that opens the gate to that garden. Trust is knowing the gardener and having the assurance that He will allow you in when you ask Him. Trust is the greatest asset God has entrusted to humanity.

True faith is not blind hope

Would you put your hope in a stranger you've never met to look after your children? If you have no record of this person's character or reliability, how can you judge that they can be trusted?

When we read Hebrews 11:11 we see the account of Sarah who put her faith in God. Scripture says she considered God faithful to deliver on His promise. The word 'faithful' is a powerful description of our main topic. To regard someone as faithful, that person must demonstrate that they can be trusted. Faith is not just blind hope that something they wish for will happen when there's no evidence that such a wish could come true. Sarah's faith can better be described as trusting God to deliver on His promise because Sarah had found God to be faithful.

Faith is therefore not blind hope nor a system of belief in something or someone without any merit. Faith is putting your hope in an undisputed truth, something that can be relied on – something that has been tested and approved. Once this truth has been affirmed, it's worthy of forming the benchmark of people's trust and it can serve as a plumb line to people's values. It's for this reason that Jesus said He is the way, the truth and the life (John 14:6). He is the undisputed value on earth, the standard God has given us, the path to eternal life. When we see that Jesus, the Word of God, fulfils all that's required to be the truth, we count Him as faithful; something to believe in and someone we can trust.

Some atheists state that Christians practice a faith that involves believing in something without any evidence. True faith is not believing in the absence of evidence – it's absolutely evidence-based. God does not ask us to believe in Him without any evidence. Romans states clearly that God has made available His visible attributes for everyone to see (Romans 1:18-20). He has placed the evidence of His existence and the incomprehensible complexity of what He created right in front of us. We not only have creation that exhibits God's existence, but we also have factual historical accounts and documented events that inform us about God throughout history. Additionally, we have subjective experiences that, to every believer, prove that God exists. The sheer complexity of humanity, their ability to design, dream, love, forgive and co-exist as families and in communities all form an undeniable argument for the existence of a good God.

Faith, having its origin with God, does not serve to accomplish natural objectives. Faith is a spiritual force and therefore its objective is always to accomplish spiritual growth. Natural objectives refer to things in our daily lives that people can do for themselves. Faith is not given to a believer to make them lazy; it doesn't detract from the command God gave to every human through Adam. Every person must work daily to provide for themselves. There are certain rules and laws within creation regarding humanity that God will not violate. People must perform their natural daily functions to remain alive and healthy.

Sin is a spiritual principle, but its effects are clearly seen in the physical. When Adam and Eve sinned, they lost the glory of God and immediately death became a reality in their natural bodies. Sin also affected the natural world as we see it decaying around us, and through God's plan of salvation, all things will be made new. Sin affected all of creation – the natural world and humanity. An important aspect of sin is that it not only affects people's natural physiological existence but it also affects their spiritual nature. God placed His Spirit in people when He created them, but when sin entered people, that aspect of God in them was corrupted. Hence, people comprise a mind, a body and a spirit, all of which were affected by sin.

For people to be restored to their former place with God where they can fully relate to Him again, a mechanism was introduced by God to solve the sin problem. Sin is a spiritual principle that can only be resisted and overcome by a spiritual force, not in the natural space. No matter how much effort people put in to right the wrongs in themselves, they're not going to be able to change their spiritual position before God.

Sin exists in people's nature and is visible in their words, actions and minds. Most importantly, humanity's sin exists before God as an accusation of guilt against them. It's for this reason that Jesus had to atone for humanity's sin.

Faith was given to people by God to enable them to be set free from sin and be re-introduced into a relationship with God. Faith therefore always opposes and resists the sinful nature within people. Faith enables the person to be reborn on the inside and to be reunited with God; it transforms the believer into a citizen worthy of the eternal city of God. The spiritual nature of faith is there to accomplish spiritual goals in people, which God has determined before the creation of what we see and know today.

Later in this book I will highlight how the enemy, as he has done with everything God created, seeks to distort faith and cause people to misuse it for personal worldly pursuits.

Chapter 4

Faith and human pursuits

F aith is a spiritual gift, given to us to achieve spiritual goals, not to fulfil our human desires and cravings. To explain what faith is not, I have included this real-life anecdote.

I recently watched a documentary of a couple who embarked on a challenging building project. The project was highly technical and the budget was three times what they could afford. Their project was to construct their dream house in a remote traditional mountain village where the local homes were constructed from large blocks of yellow stone from nearby hills. The couple's design featured glass, steel and concrete, to the disgust of the local people. The couple went ahead with their project and on completion it was way over budget and far beyond its original timeline. In their desire to fulfil their dream, the couple made many enemies. At the end of the documentary, the presenter explained how both the husband and wife accomplished their dream by using their "faith". He said that no bank was willing to lend them money for their building project so it was up to the husband to transform his business to find the necessary funds to initiate and complete their project. It was said that he used his so-called faith in his business skills to generate funding for the house project. The wife, as it was explained, used her faith in designing a cost-effective environment-friendly structure.

This story highlights what true faith is and what it is not.

Through human persistence, tenacity and hard work, this couple was successful in their endeavours. But was it the couple's faith that accomplished their project, or was it mere human effort, hard work and skills? Were they believers and if so, did they consult God regarding their dream? Did God approve the messy relations with their neighbours and the community as a whole? Did God allow the severe debt they found themselves in post-completion? What part of the house could be attributed to their salvation and subsequent holiness?

Make no mistake, humanity is powerful. Created as God's representative and manager on earth and created in His likeness, despite their fall and the consequent curses, they can achieve great feats. This was already displayed in Genesis 11 when people, using their God-given talents and skills, built the first skyscraper.

The story of the couple who planned and built their dream house is the same as the people who built the Tower of Babel. No faith was used in either the planning or the construction of the two projects.

People's cleverness will accomplish many things, but their achievements may not be in line with God's will at the time. In fact, many believers might achieve great feats, yet while they labour in their projects, they could be in total disobedience of God's commands and will for them.

Faith is not what we can do, but what we can lay down before God. It's a spiritual gift to accomplish spiritual goals, not human endeavours. When faith is misappropriated, it never glorifies God. It always elevates the flesh and distracts those involved and those looking on. When this couple constructed their home, they did not use faith at all. It was their combined human abilities they employed to accomplish their personal dream. Faith had nothing to do with it. It was human effort, knowledge and determination that finished the project, not faith. As the presenter rightfully said: 'They believed in themselves and their dream.' It had nothing to do with God's will for their lives. Their human endeavour, in this case, was void of God's Word because God's Word will always avoid the flesh being glorified. This couple's project was a fleshly drive to fulfil a fleshly desire.

False teachings

Christians have fallen victim to many similar false teachings since the creation of the world. One of the more recent false teachings is the "faith movement", which focuses on faith as a tool for the believer to achieve prosperity on earth. This teaching has sparked a "grab all you can" drive among wealthy western churches; faith is promoted apart from the other spiritual principles every believer is called to master.

When faith is taught as a wealth-creation tool, it has veered off course from what it was meant to achieve. Faith initiates the reconciliation process God has begun on earth through His Son Jesus. By dying on the cross, being buried and raised on the third day, Jesus has enabled every believer to enter an eternal relationship with God. When faith is isolated and abused, it causes a believer to misuse the spiritual gift God made available to a dying world. Whenever in doubt, see if what you want to employ faith for fits into the person and work of Jesus Christ.

Another misnomer when it comes to faith is when people try the mind-over-matter approach. In this psychological step into the dark, a person keeps saying something subjective to themselves over and over until they eventually believe that it is true or achievable. This mind trick is void of any spirituality and has caused great hurt to many people. Faith requires a surrender to God by the person, like the woman with the issue of blood who by then had sought help from many doctors, but in vain. She reached the end of her efforts and surrendered to Jesus (Luke 8:43,44). Mind-over-matter is not a surrender, but a sinful elevation of the person's human abilities.

Believers fall into traps when they begin to walk by subjective truth, which is when a person reads a portion of Scripture that promises good things and then chooses to believe what that portion says but ignores the context of the verse. To such people, what they've read is God's Word – and yes, it might be His Word, but it's not all He said. This subjective truth can happen when a person "claims" a Bible verse for themselves without respecting the Scriptural context, but God is not a vending machine where we stick some token in and our greatest desire pops out. Objective truth, on the other hand, is achieved when we follow all the proper Bible interpretation steps.

In most cases, Scripture contains conditional blessings. When believers apply subjective truth, they clam the blessings or benefits mentioned in the verses but fail to fulfil the required conditions. Countless heresies have emerged when believers "apply" Scripture verses out of context.

In Jesus' time, the Pharisees diligently studied the Scripture expecting to obtain life from it, but the written Word alone cannot bring life. Only the person of Jesus Christ can bring life, and it's our faith in Him that regenerates our spirits. Cold compliance with commands is not what God desires from us. He desires a relationship whereby we obey Him and trust Him because of the love He has shown us. The world is full of pseudo-faith movements whereby so-called believers expect eternal life by observing a set of rules. Jesus came to break this fallacy by saying He wants people to come to Him for life and not try to obtain life through blind obedience to a set of rules (John 5:39,40). Pseudo-faith is when people rigidly follow a set of rules and expect to be approved before God. Faith is not a ritualised religious practice. Faith is attached to a person in whom we have placed our trust.

Faith is not the abuse of a spiritual gift to achieve personal self-enrichment. Faith is part of the inner workings of a relationship of trust with God the Father, Son and Holy Spirit. A believer who claims to walk by faith but does not have the love of the Father, nor Scriptural context or sensitivity to the Spirit is walking in human strength, not faith.

Ignorance in believers

To many believers who've been saved by grace though faith according to the Ephesians 2:8,9, faith was not very tangible or understood at the moment they were born again. What takes place thereafter is that the person begins their spiritual journey. It may even seem as if faith was just momentarily needed as a once-off event. The contrary is true.

For in the gospel the righteousness of God is revealed—a

righteousness that is by faith from first to last, just as it is written: 'The righteous will live by faith.' Romans 1:17 (NIV)

Here Paul says that living by faith must be a focus for every believer, and that it is faith that develops the believer from one level to the next.

Many believers seem to show ignorance about God's requirement that they need to live by faith. This absence of applied faith in their lives means that they embark on manmade projects and deeds in an effort to impress God. But unless their deeds are founded on faith they will not be approved by God. Ephesians 2:10 speaks of the good deeds performed by the believer, but these are works that are pre-planned for the believer by God. They are not deeds thought up by the believer, nor did the believer require trust in God to perform them. They were designed and executed by God in a believer's wisdom and strength and therefore they warrant no reward by God. This takes us back to the essence of faith, which is trust in God and allowing Him to control everything. Faith is a process whereby a person lays down their worth and shows their dependence on God, acknowledging their weakness and inviting God's power.

Believers who practice a pseudo-faith achieve certain goals by mixing faith and their own deeds. They trust God up to a point, but maintain a safe back-door policy if things don't work out. They use Scripture but fuse it with manmade ideas and philosophies. They start on a journey of faith, trusting God, but when things get tough they abandon that plan and turn to plan B, drawing on resources other than God to bail them out. God does not desire a fifty per cent loyalty from the believer; He demands it all. A person's wisdom and strength can never be fused with God's Word to obtain supernatural empowerment and provision.

A lack of Biblical understanding will cause believers to walk in a mixture of their own and God's wisdom and power; they're likely to try to "force" the hand of God to achieve a particular goal.

True faith, not blind faith

When listening to a leading atheist recently, I heard the term "blind faith". He was stating that Christianity was an absurd worldview because everything is based on the Christian faith, which he termed a blind faith. He was saying that Christians believe in theories without any evidence.

Well, the Apostle Paul addressed this clearly in Romans 1:

> The wrath of God is being revealed from heaven against all the godlessness and wickedness of people, who suppress the truth by their wickedness, since what may be known about God is plain to them, because God has made it plain to them. For since the creation of the world God's invisible qualities—his eternal power and divine nature—have been clearly seen, being understood from what has been made, so that people are without excuse. Romans 1:18-20 (NIV)

Paul said that God's invisible qualities can be seen in what He made – in the incredible complexities found in the universe. Paul also said that God made Himself visible in creation so that people are without an excuse.

In Exodus 19:4-6 God reminded Israel how He had brought them out of Egyptian slavery; He was giving them evidential markers to hold onto as they walked from Mount Sinai into the unknown Wilderness towards the Promised Land. This reminder was to assist the Israelites to put their trust in God in future because He had fulfilled every promise He made. The evidence they could anchor their faith on was what God had done for them. God told them that He was willing and able to do for them again what He had done when liberating them from Egypt. He was making a case that He could be trusted to liberate them from slavery, to walk with them through the Wilderness, and to take them across the Jordan River to inhabit the Promised Land. Every time they looked back to see what God had done for them before, they were strengthened in their faith. God showed Himself as historically trustworthy and He can therefore be trusted by every believer.

In John 14:11 Jesus told the people to believe in Him because of the miracles He performed.

> Believe me when I say that I am in the Father and the
> Father is in me; or at least believe on the evidence of the
> works themselves. John 14:11 (NIV)

He was making a link between His miraculous provision of food for the masses and God's provision of everything the Israelites needed in their Wilderness journey. It is therefore not blind faith that Jesus asked His followers through to us today to have in Him. It's true faith.

An assurance of what you believe in

One of the reasons I chose the title for this book was to give the reader an assurance of what they believe in. I want them to know that what they have placed their trust in is believable and reliable. This is not blind faith, as the atheist referred to earlier stated, claiming that Christians place their faith in a God who does not exist.

The believer's faith is in the existence of a God who lives in the heart of every believer and who has revealed Himself through His visible attributes to all people (Romans 1:20). God's actions have been documented since the creation of the world and everything we can see. There are several powerful arguments to refute unbelief when someone claims God does not exist:

- If God does not exist, what is the opposite argument for who created the universe with all its complexities, perfect timing and the brilliance of man's creativity?
- If the universe is a garden, perfectly shaped and maintained, then who is the gardener? Surely something this spectacular and perfect must have been created by someone infinitely more spectacular and perfect? If you eat a mango it can only be from a mango tree – fruit does not exist by itself.

To deny that God exists is to place humanity in an eternal predicament. Not only are people unable to exist independent of their creator, but they're also faced with the undeniable visible evidence that surrounds them every day. If God does not exist, then the question is, in what will people place their hope and where can they look for answers to their problems? Is humanity's answer locked away within themselves? People need a saviour outside of themselves; a saviour who is eternally true, eternally holy and always righteous.

Agnostics and atheists may argue against the existence of God; they may quote the theories of Charles Darwin regarding evolution. What none of these God-denialists can explain is the origin of life and who created it. When a believer puts their trust in God and His Word, they put their hope in the One who created the universe and also sustains it in perfect working order. Scientists have calculated that should the force of gravity change by even a small margin, everything in the universe would collapse. The God we place our trust in formed the universe and He put in place every law and constant to maintain it in perfect order. So I say again: if a person walks in a forest and finds a perfectly maintained garden, they will automatically assume there is a gardener. Similarly, should a person look up at the night sky and see the billions of stars, they will automatically assume there is a creator. It is more plausible to accept that creation has a creator than to believe that it all came into existence from a big bang. There is no opposing argument that can be presented to prove that anything other than God created the universe and everything in it.

Chapter 5

Why not faith?

I magine if a qualified surgeon chose not to use medical equipment and prescribed medical procedures during a complicated operation. He would risk the life and wellbeing of his patients and would likely be struck off the medical register. As an excuse for his conduct, he could say that he knows what he's doing and he will keep on trying to perfect his work until he has evidence to prove his case, ignoring the authority of the medical board. But ignoring sound medical procedures would only spell disaster for the surgeon and his patients – abiding by the rules of medicine is not the surgeon's choice; it's a statutory requirement.

This scenario may sound absurd, but this is how many believers live their Christian lives on earth. They're qualified to be Christians by means of God's grace through faith. However, they choose to live their lives completely without God, and in many cases, against God's will, ignoring His ways and rejecting His commands. For many believers, living by their own strength and applying their own wisdom seems the right way to go. After all, this is what they relied on for many years before their salvation.

People are created in God's own likeness (Genesis 1:26), which means that people have incredible creative abilities, great resilience and a wealth of knowledge to accomplish great tasks. This suggests that believers who depend on their own strength seem successful on the surface. They're quick to show off their achievements and feel empowered to celebrate their own human achievements. This is done in total ignorance of God's expectation regarding His gift of faith to human beings. Scripture makes it clear that none of humanity's achievements have any value in God's eyes unless they are done through faith.

Living by faith has interesting applications. Hebrews 11:6 says faith is first a requirement to approach God to receive His rewards. Second, faith is a command in Scripture that the righteous shall walk or live by (Romans 1:17). Third, faith is a spiritual application to achieve supernatural assistance where it is needed to supersede specific natural circumstances. Fourth, faith is a gift of God to all of humanity, which sets aside all human boasting. Faith requires people to surrender all their talents, trophies, abilities, wisdom and strength and approach God for what they themselves are unable to do. Fifth, faith is a spiritual application, therefore the physical and mental realms that people operate in are bypassed.

Faith does not require people to completely set aside their abilities. It only requires that they bring them under God's authority. Humans can accomplish many things, but their initial surrender before God to ask what the correct way forward might be, allows God to bless their efforts in using their God-given talents, trophies, abilities, wisdom and strength. Faith therefore does not nullify people's God-given abilities; it empowers them to prosper.

Where is your faith?

After rebuking the wind and raging waters, Jesus asked His disciples, 'Where is your faith?' (Luke 8:25). Remember that these men were seasoned fishermen. Jesus' question was more a rhetorical one than a rebuke. He was drawing an answer out of them to show them how to accomplish what normal fishermen in their situation could not. It would have been unfair for Jesus to expect them to stand up and rebuke the storm because they had not yet been trained to do so. However, Jesus stood up with authority over the natural elements as an example of what faith can accomplish.

Ask yourself, so why not faith? Why should any believer walk this road on their own? Why should believers, who are a target of the enemy's pursuits, fight their battles in their own strength? Why would a believer disregard God's laws, His ways and a free offer of supernatural assistance? Why not appeal to the creator of heaven and earth for help? Why not surrender your God-given talents, trophies, abilities, wisdom and strength to God and receive the supernatural empowering for what He has called you to do?

God commands every person to make a daily living, but He also calls the believer to do great exploits for the Kingdom of God. Why go it alone when you can obey God and reap the benefits?

In Luke 8:25 we can see why Jesus asked His disciples the famous question. He was not unreasonable in His expectation of them, He was saying that there's something available to help them accomplish life and what He had called them to. He wanted them to see beyond the natural, beyond their own limited experience and wisdom. He wanted these fishermen to become fishers of men. To do this, they would need more than mental and physical strength; they would need supernatural empowering – faith (Matthew 4:19; Acts 1:8).

Later in this book we tackle the issue of why believers still rely on themselves and not on God. This disposition can be seen as humanity's greatest weakness; it's the result of disobedience and their subsequent fall mentioned in Genesis 3:5.

Chapter 6

Humanity's desperate need

To fully understand God's plan of salvation, we must clearly distinguish the components it's made up of, such as grace, mercy, justification, the new birth, total forgiveness, sanctification, the removal of sin, Jesus as the Atoning Lamb of God, the work of the Holy Spirit and many more. However, there's a key element that makes all these components a reality – which is faith. It's the aspect we see from Genesis to Revelation that enables God's plan of salvation from the start all the way to fruition. To understand faith, we need to ask some important questions. Why did God give people the gift of faith? Can people generate their own faith? Is faith the same as willpower? Is a human being born with a sense of or the primary seeds of faith? Can faith be a learnt experience? Does Scripture state clearly where faith originates?

Faith, when put into practice, can be expressed as "to believe". Jesus Himself used the words faith and trust interchangeably (John 14:1 and Luke 18:8). Most dictionaries define faith as a complete trust or confidence in someone or something; a strong belief in the doctrines of a religion based on spiritual conviction rather than proof. It's interesting that these definitions mention "conviction" as more important than "proof". In Jesus' own words, seeing is not believing.

Faith is the trust we place in a person and this trust exists before the person has fulfilled their actual promise to us. Faith or trust is therefore an anchor we rely on and it should not be placed in something or someone before we have confirmed their trustworthiness. Only when we have accumulated, verified and objectively confirmed such evidence, can we say the person or thing has a proven track record. Paul states this in Romans 1: 19,20, and God proved His faithfulness to Israel, as explained in Isaiah 46:3,4. God is not a man that He would lie.

We've all seen incredible feats of engineering such as suspension bridges built to connect two previously disconnected landmasses, making it possible for people and cargo to travel back and forth. The stronger the bridge is, the heavier the load it can bear. Similarly, relationships are social engineering feats that can bear incredible weight, and faith can be described as a suspension bridge of trust that God has built between Himself and human beings. His aim is to use this bridge to restore people to Himself.

The picture of the suspension bridge between God and people shows that people need to reach God but are unable to do so using their own efforts, wisdom and knowledge. If people could shake off their sins and restore their broken relationship with God by using their own knowledge and wisdom, they would have done so long ago. However, the mistake people make is that they regard sin from their own broken point of view instead of regarding holiness from God's point of view. Those people who committed the sin, cannot be the same ones who can restore what they have broken. Only God could resolve humanity's predicament – which is dealing with their sinful nature. Only God can rid a person of their rebellious nature and instil a God-like nature. Only God can empower a person to desire what is holy and pure. Only God can make a person love their enemies. In fact, God's commands are practically impossible for people to uphold all the time, but we see in Scripture that what God expects of people cannot be performed by them in their own strength or wisdom. People need a power or an enabling from God to live up to God's standard.

Sin has blinded people's reasoning by introducing an arrogant belief that they're able to save themselves from their own predicament (2 Corinthians 4:4). Humanity's greatest need is a force working to enable them to reach out for help that is not within themselves, but from an external source. If people, as in the days of Babel (Genesis 11), could locate a source of power within themselves to renew their fallen nature, they would be a god unto themselves.

This is the reason that the Tree of the knowledge of good and evil came with a prohibition in Genesis 2. Humanity's arrogance originated from the false sense of superiority in that they see God from their own perspective. God is eternally and infinitely holy, pure and righteous. This is His standard for Himself and the whole of creation – which includes all people. There is therefore no act, pledge, sacrifice or deed that people could perform to redeem themselves to God's standard. Any process initiated to restore people to God's standard of holiness has to originate with God Himself.

This is made clear in Philippians 2:5-11. The process God initiated to reconcile people back to Himself in a holy relationship cannot begin with people themselves. It must be a process both planned and executed by God Himself.

I believe this is exactly what we read in John 3:16. God personally planned and executed His own plan. We also see the blueprint for humanity's participation in this plan. There exists only one possible way people can enter and benefit from this eternal plan of God; the only way fallen people can be reconciled to God is by faith. This principle is clearly seen in both the Old and New Testament (Genesis 15:6 and Ephesians 2:8-9).

Faith begins with surrender

Faith begins with a person's surrender. They need to come to the feet of Jesus to be justified, sanctified and finally glorified. What God expects of people in the spiritual realm is totally impossible for them to accomplish; it's easier to understand what God expects of people when looking at the principle of spiritual warfare. Ephesians 6:12 says that our fight is not against flesh and blood, but against spiritual principalities. What Paul is saying is that traditional weapons are of no use here. Come to Jesus, put your weapons down and learn how to fight in the spirit. This is a process where the old fleshly methods are laid down and a person learns a totally new way of life.

The three steps:
First, faith touches a person at the point of their being justified (Romans 5:1; Ephesians 2:8).

Second, faith helps a person to meet their daily needs and in protecting them from physical harm (Matthew 6:33; Hebrews 1:14).

Third, faith is the only thing a person has when they close their eyes for the last time to be with God forever – when they depart from this world to enter another (Hebrews 13:14).

When we see how some American televangelists have twisted the purpose of faith, it should cause us to revisit why God gave people the gift of faith in the first place. A prominent pastor once said that after he read that God made Abraham extremely rich, he became very interested in being rich himself.

This pastor, a leader in the faith movement, and his teachings seem to advocate the use of faith as a tool to gain worldly wealth. This teaching has clearly departed far from God giving faith to humanity as a gift. God made Abraham rich, not because of Abraham's faith, but because of his obedience that followed his faith. Genesis 24:35 refers to Abraham's riches clearly as building up after Abraham displayed his obedience to God in Genesis 17:1.

Who controls whom?

It's important to have a good understanding of the gifts of the Holy Spirit. Paul makes the statement that we are to be controlled by the Spirit (Romans 8:9). Something is wrong with how some pastors approach the use of the gifts they've received from the Holy Spirit. It seems as if they've received a gift from the Spirit and use it even to "command" the Spirit to come and go as and when they choose. Paul tells the believer that the Spirit of God is there to lead us in our walk with God; we're to keep in step with Him and not Him with us (Galatians 5:25). When a believer begins to dictate to the Spirit, the gift becomes the object and the relationship the believer has with the Spirit is neglected. No relationship can thrive when one party wants to dominate.

The nine gifts of the Spirit in the church (1 Corinthian 12) are for the common good, not for one person only. When receiving a gift from the Spirit, it should be given away in the church for the benefit of others. Many believers incorrectly hold onto this gift and seize it to be used when they choose to. They even begin to develop this gift to make it seem as if they control it. As if this is not enough, they command the Spirit to make the gift work when they choose. But the essential aspect of faith is not that it is to be applied as a tool towards achievement.

Humanity is in trouble because of sin. They have no way of rescuing themselves by any means; they're caught in a position where they're not in right-standing with God. Sin has caused a great divide between people and God and the only way this can be remedied is by receiving God's gift of grace. People must surrender to be rescued and forgiven, and without surrender, they will retain their arrogant stand against God and they will not receive God's pardon.

Receiving a gift from God should always be respected and treated as a gift, because a surrendered heart is a safe place where God can place His gifts. This means that the believer who has a surrendered heart, as David did, will allow the Spirit to lead them. They will be guided by the Spirit about how and when the gifts they have received must be applied, and they understand the relationship they have with the Spirit. God's will is for His Spirit to control the use of the gifts He bestows on believers and no believer should regard a gift they've received from the Spirit as a way to enhance their public profile or advance their personal goals.

Nothing else will do

One of my all-time favourite Christian bands is Delirious from the United Kingdom. They produced a song called 'Solid Rock', which has the following lyrics:

> On Christ the solid rock we will stand.
> All other ground is sinking sand.

From the beginning of time this has been true. In our turbulent world you can find endless sources of information, free advice and instant answers on almost every imaginable topic, certainly more than anyone could read in a lifetime. But what can be believed?

When studying theology, we come across the authority, the sufficiency and the authenticity of Scripture. It answers questions such as, 'Why do we as Christians believe Scripture is authoritative, inerrant, alive and inspired?' As any good defence attorney will tell you, useful evidence must be able to withstand all kinds of scrutiny to be deemed trustworthy.

Evidence for the existence of God is not only contained in Scripture; proof that God exists comes to us via Scripture where it says we can observe God's handywork in creation all around us. He has made His invisible qualities – His eternal power and divine nature – for all to see (Romans 1:20). God's handywork in creating humans and the vast universe that runs on millisecond perfection after millions of years are testimony that no one can argue against.

Where can a person find truth when they need to navigate the uncertainties we face daily? What source of information can be relied on when so many sources of so-called reliable information need regular updates. What evidence is available to the believer that has passed the most rigorous scrutiny? Is there a set of rules a believer can shape their life around that was produced by a higher power, a pure power, an uncompromised person?

The only source of reliable, unchanging, inerrant and eternal information is the Bible. In the Canon of Scripture, people can learn about their origin, the reason for the state of the planet and where they will find themselves in a million years from now.

There are as many sources as there are other religions, ideologies or belief systems and it's easy to get lost in this confusion. One of the things that sets the Bible apart from any other religion, is that its source is not people. Jesus, the Word, was from the beginning and existed before the creation of the world. Jesus Himself is eternal and is fully God, even though He was incarnated as a man on earth. His words were the words of God Himself, given to Him by His Father (John 12:49). They are eternal, pure, inerrant and always true. When a believer wants to place their trust in something that is true and reliable, nothing else will do. Only God's words contained in Scripture and inspired by the Spirit of God can be trusted. Faith can only be true when it is backed up by truth – placing your trust in a source of information that has no credibility deems all your efforts worthless from the start.

Chapter 7

Mistakes many believers make

J esus said to Simon Peter: 'Launch into the deep' (Luke 5:4-5). Nothing Jesus said made sense to the rational mind. Peter knew that daytime fishing near the shoreline made no sense. His whole experiential framework was challenged by what Jesus said; he'd been fishing all night and caught nothing. Why would he disregard natural science and many years of experience and obey Jesus in a space that was his home ground? Here we begin to see how psychology and faith are mutually exclusive. Jesus' command required Peter to set aside rational thinking and fully rely on what Jesus said. In Peter's case, it was not relying on what was said, but rather who said it. He made the following remark: 'Master, we have toiled all the night, and have taken nothing; nevertheless, at thy word I will let down the net' (Luke 5:5).

How faith differs from psychology

In most situations, when stress and anxiety grow in a person's mind, it requires something to happen to deflect their mind away from the current problem. Compare this to faith, which allows God to step in when He decides and provide what the person needs. The waiting period involved can be the one aspect God uses to challenge our thinking. From Biblical examples and personal experience, God does not function in line with our psychological attributes; His ways are higher than our ways. His plans are often either delayed or not what we expect, yet they're always perfect in timing and they always accomplish more than we could ask or dream.

Our minds are the obstacles stopping us from surrendering to God and allowing Him to take charge and solve our problems. In human terms, our minds want immediate answers, using fleshly ways and human wisdom. Faith challenges our minds to surrender our inner voices of reason and experience. If we are to see a demonstration of God's power and faithfulness, we need to set aside the arguments in our minds. In the Gospels, Jesus often operated above and beyond the realm of science, reason and social practices.

The definition of faith says we need to close our eyes and trust God. He has repeatedly proven Himself faithful. But ignoring our inner voice of reason is easier said than done. As did doubting Thomas, we first want to see how it all will work out before we will invest (John 20:25). Up to the point of salvation, we have lived by our own strength and wisdom. When we surrendered our lives to Jesus this all stopped and from that point, we need to unlearn doing things our own way. Paul says our minds need to be renewed – we need to do away with the natural way of reasoning and bring in the new way of spiritual thinking (Romans 12:2). Our biggest challenge is laying down our efforts and the thoughts that oppose Jesus' commands (1 Corinthians 2:5). This is where our psychological framework wants to oppose the knowledge of

God. What we can see has been our stronghold, but now faith bypasses our visual attributes and replaces them with trust in God's Word and we shift from self-reliance to the denial of self (Matthew 16:24).

Returning to what's easy

After the Israelites departed from 400 years of slavery in Egypt, God met with them in person at Mount Sinai for the first time. Trust is the most important aspect in any relationship and one of the most challenging things for any believer is to reach a place where we hand over control to God, surrendering and placing our hand in His. It sounds easier than it is. Handing over control to God after being in slavery for 400 years was also not easy. Although Israel had agreed to trust God and despite all the signs and wonders He had performed, when difficulties arose, they defaulted to the gods they embraced in Egypt.

Both Jesus and the author of Hebrews warned that difficulties will come and will either develop or erode our trust in God and His Word.

Just as Israel did, we find it hard to hand over control to God. We revert to what we do easily, which is to make things happen when we need to. It's not easy to wait for God to show up and provide. Not only do we have our own history, values and abilities driving us to perform, but we also have the inherent disbelieving and doubtful mindsets we inherited from Adam. To hand over our past, present and future decisions to God is a greater challenge than the average believer has faced in the past. We easily call Jesus our Saviour and we appreciate his grace, but when it comes to Jesus' designated role as Lord, we are slow to follow Him. Lord-ship requires a person to submit – to hand over control and lay down your will – and to become a disciple means exactly this. You place your trust in Jesus and count everything else a loss for His name's sake. Placing your life in someone else's hands is a volitional decision. As Christians, we tend to attempt it once or twice, but we do so reluctantly, and while we place our trust into His capable hands, we also hold onto it just in case it doesn't go as we envisaged or expected. If it doesn't, we become impatient. We say we surrender, but we ensure we remain in command.

Even Jesus' closest followers were challenged with trusting Him. After Jesus ascended to His place next to the Father, He must have left a big void where once He had walked with His disciples. When Jesus called Peter he was a fisherman and was used to his daily routine of fishing. Jesus came and took him out of his comfort zone and called him to ministry. When Jesus left, Peter decided to return to his family's fishing nets and boats as the place that he could control. He could decide to do anything he wanted and was accountable to no one but himself.

Chapter 8

Put down your calculator

The ordinary things and methods in this world work according to scientific and mathematical calculations and people use these calculations to plan their lives by. From the beginning of time, people observed the stars to plan for what was coming and today they build powerful computer systems to analyse data to predict what will happen tomorrow. People put their trust in what they can create.

However, the very Person Jesus asked the Father to send us after He ascended to heaven is the Holy Spirit. He is a Person in the Trinity and He was also part of the creation of everything seen and unseen. He exists in a realm far beyond the basic principles of this world. God the Father has given us His Spirit to give us eternal life, to lead and guide us in this world. By obeying His voice, we can touch the realm He exists in. When we begin to live by the Spirit, we begin to operate on a new level where the wisdom, knowledge and talents of humanity fall short. Scripture says that the wisdom people use is often in conflict with the wisdom of the Spirit (1 Corinthians 3:19). When a person is indwelt by the Person of the Spirit of God, they must begin to walk in the power of the Spirit (Galatians 5:25; Galatians 3:1-5). The Spirit enables the believer to live on earth in a way that resembles heaven.

A person filled with the Spirit of God has surrendered their wisdom, will and expectations and by doing so, they're empowered with Godly wisdom, knowledge and power. To the measure the believer surrenders to the Spirit, they can be empowered by the Spirit. This is what Jesus taught His disciples when He said that with the measure they use to understand His teachings, it will be measured back to them (Mark 4:24). This is why the salvation plan of God found in the death, burial and resurrection of Jesus is received by faith only. Faith is a spiritual gift that allows people to do what they cannot do for themselves.

When it comes to the application of faith, reducing ourselves, our very claim to self-reliance, can be seen as humbling ourselves. In faith terms, this means laying down the basic principles of this world, which is required before we can experience the Spirit's power. As long as we keep trying to achieve the impossible in our own strength, the Spirit will not act on our behalf. He wants to enter through the door of invitation into our lives, but we can prevent Him from entering by standing in the doorway.

To live by the Spirit requires that we walk by the Spirit, using faith in God as our foundation. Without faith, people will look to themselves for what they cannot achieve or correct in themselves. Using their own wisdom, they will never step into the spiritual realm where they draw on the Spirit's power to deliver what only the Spirit can achieve on their behalf.

The account of David counting his mighty men in 1 Samuel 24 is a clear example of people employing the basic principles of this world to try to achieve the impossible. David wanted to calculate and assure himself that what God promised was feasible. Like David, those who trust in their own wisdom and strength are constantly calculating and relying on themselves as the source of their power and provision. God gave David a job to do. David had to surrender his own wisdom and trust God to help him but David initially calculated the fighting men available to him. He replaced the Almighty God with the ability of his fighting men. David wanted to do the impossible using the possible. We might call David's act a mistake, but God called it sin. David was punished for his sin and 70,000 men died.

The account of Jesus inviting the rich young man to follow Him was a testament to how hard it is for someone to abandon their safe harbour and join Jesus in the rough seas (Matthew 19:16-22). What Jesus offered him made no sense to the businessman's calculations. Jesus spoke of eternal wealth while the young man thought only of worldly wealth.

When we as believers do calculations to achieve spiritual things, it is offensive to the Spirit of God. It is natural for us to initially feel anxious as soon as we step out of what we're used to. Our comfort zones and calculators give us a sense of security. It's at this point that we should allow the Spirit to take over and do the impossible. For as long as people use their calculators, namely their own wisdom and reasoning, they're blind to spiritual things. When people lay down their calculator, the Spirit empowers them to see in the realm of the Spirit.

One and not the other

Have you ever seen a bodybuilder who, from the knees up, looks impressive, but doesn't have much to show in their calves. This is because some of the hardest muscles to develop are the calves. A person could be exceptionally developed in their upper body, but it could appear as if they'd skipped leg-day! Their physiques look out of balance and they'll never be able to win a competition until they can bring their calves into balance with the rest of their bodies.

For many believers, operating in the gift of faith can resemble that of an unbalanced bodybuilder. Scripture speaks of the physical and spiritual body of the believer. Imagine the believer has large "faith" shoulders, but no "patience" calves. The gift of faith is one of the nine gifts the Spirit gives (1 Corinthians 12:9) and patience is one of the nine fruits of the Spirit (Ephesians 5:22-23). Patience is painstakingly developed over long periods and is a true character development boot-camp experience.

Many believers begin to walk by faith using the gift of the Spirit. However, many ignore patience as a fruit of the Spirit. Not having patience as a balance in the believer's spiritual body makes them unbalanced. This means they embark on faith projects and demand to see their prayers answered immediately. Failure to experience immediate gratification can leave the believer pointing fingers at God.

We often read in Scripture about Abraham, the man of faith. Yes, indeed, Abraham has been singled out as the first person in Scripture to be saved by faith (Genesis 15:6). We also see in Scripture that Abraham became concerned about his and Sarah's old age. Abraham agreed with Sarah to create his own solution to the ageing problem (Genesis 16:1-4) and he had a son with Hagar to secure his lineage. This was a desperate act of being impatient. God had promised, but Abraham was swayed by what he saw and calculated.

Like Abraham, many believers walk by faith, but fail to develop a faith that is balanced with patience. It's like choosing one of the gifts of the Spirit and developing it to a high level while at the same time patience as a fruit of the Spirit is ignored. Today there are many so-called faith preachers who relish the applause they get from their acts of faith. When an overemphasis is placed on faith, the believer's life will show signs of distortion.

Clinging to the pilot seat

In the beginning God created Adam and Eve because it was God's aim to have people to fellowship with. He gave them a free will and He also gave Adam work to do. Adam's free will allowed him to either obey or disobey God's commands; it had boundaries and the main one was obedience, which was designed to keep him safe. Adam's actions would set the tone for every human born after him because he was given the role as representative for humanity.

Obeying God was the key to Adam remaining under God's covering. To any believer, submission is an expression of obedience to God's will and His ways. It's also a way of expressing trust in God because obedience to God's commands shows an understanding that God created and maintains everything.

After sinning, Adam lost the wisdom of God, which means that everything he did was by his own flawed human rationale. By remaining within his God-given boundaries, Adam would be living within the favour of God. The enemy of God, the serpent, knew this well. Adam lived under God's covering and the way the jealous serpent could attack God's man was to get him to question the validity and benefits of this covering. To get Adam to wilfully step out from within God's authority, the serpent had to lie to him. People were created to be dependent on their creator, which was the very focus of the enemy's lie. The two trees in the Garden of Eden represented either a submissive existence and harmony with God or a rebellions pursuit of autonomous self-governance, and God placed them in the garden as a sign of man's free will. The one carried the blessing of eternal life and freedom, the other eternal death and suffering.

How did the enemy attract man's attention to consider the possibility of self-governance? The serpent proposed a way whereby Adam and Eve could step away from God; they would purportedly have sovereign control over their destiny. The serpent painted the picture that the man and woman could achieve a God-like existence, governing and sustaining themselves indefinitely.

True faith means that a person gives God control of their life through a trust relationship with Him. By doing this they're under God's covering where they enjoy God's provision and protection. God did not create people to dominate and control them in an abusive and authoritative way. This is evident in that fact that God gave man a free will to decide for themselves. God wanted people to trust Him, which was expressed by obeying Him.

Rules were there to keep people safe, not hinder or harm them. By trusting God fully and submitting to Him, people are assured that God is for them and wants the best for them.

Today this root of taking control of our lives is seen in almost everything we do as humans. When it comes to the life of a believer, the control aspect becomes far more important.

The Biblical way of being born again is to be saved by grace through faith. This is a process through which a person declares their inability to change their eternal destiny and reaches out to God to take control of their life. Although people reach out to God in this way, they often later want to remain in control of their own lives – but Christians are both renewed by faith and are to walk by faith, according to the Apostle Paul. This means we trust God to renew us and we trust Him to provide for us and to protect us.

To be saved or renewed by faith is an instantaneous once-off event, but living by faith is a daily volitional laying down of our will and following Jesus. It means getting out of the pilot seat and allowing Him to take control of our lives. Let me warn you that it's easier said than done. Taking up Jesus' cross of obedience is not an easy step. It requires that we pass the same test Adam failed in Genesis. Relinquishing control requires putting to death the fleshly desires of the fallen human nature we inherited from Adam.

Before God can ascend to the throne in a person's life, He requires that such a person chooses to allow Him to control what we do and what we say and think. After all, why would we not benefit when the creator is in charge? It sounds illogical to even think otherwise. Unfortunately, few believers are willing to relinquish the pilot seat in their own airplane; they haven't relinquished control, nor have they submitted their lives to God's leading. They might have been born again, but daily they resist His commands. Romans 8:14 says that those who understand the leading of God and the benefits it brings can be described as children of God. Paul then describes the difference between being children and being a slave. The one means benefitting from voluntarily allowing God to control our lives by His Spirit, while the other refers to suffering at someone else's hand without the hope of ever changing the outcome.

It's a hard thing for a person to hand over control of their lives and trust God. The moment they get to the place of surrendering the cockpit to God, the enemy whispers the same lie he told Adam. Why should you let God tell you what to do? He only wants to limit your life and make you miserable. Stay in charge and maintain control; this way you can pursue your future goals and plans.

Chapter 9

The stakes are too high

I t's clear in Scripture that God prepares an individual for a task ahead of time. Sometimes the task is to take up a leadership role, which is preceded by the individual being discipled and prepared for the task in a type of in-process training that can include a series of test or trails. These are not always planned, because leadership training often includes the pruning of character and heart.

This time of preparation is never an easy or pleasant time because a leadership position requires that everything that's not in place when the process starts, must be dealt with. Any defects left until after the person is deployed to lead will cause them pain. If a person is deployed when not ready, their failures are seen in the open and affect others. They and sometimes those they lead get hurt when their leadership flaws are addressed. It's therefore critical that a person being prepared for leadership should not be released prematurely. The stakes are just too high.

The reason that premature release is unfortunate is because any person being prepared for a great task will often be enticed into taking a pre-emptive "promotion" by the enemy, which is not from God. It's designed to focus on the desires of the flesh to cause the individual to step out of God's plan. It happens so easily because it is the desired outcome – in the mind of the person. It looks genuine and its timing is normally exact, but taking the promotion will cause a derailment of the person's wellbeing. The promotion is designed to elevate the person's ego and reduce their dependence on God's wisdom, His appointment and His anointing. It causes the person to deviate from God's path and timing into personal ambition and the desire for public prominence. In these cases, God's blessing is not with the person. The so-called promotion may start well, seemingly successfully, but in a short space of time the wheels come off. Hurt follows quickly and can be permanent, which are the outcomes when a person does not have God's blessings for a particular leadership appointment.

During a time of testing, their lacuna, which means a missing part, becomes evident. It will become obvious that they lack the necessary training or experience to deal with issues on a leadership level.

David in the Cave of Adullam

We read about David's encounter in the Cave of Adullam (1 Samuel 24:1-22) when his pursuer, King Saul, came to relieve himself in the cave. David had the opportunity to kill his pursuer, and one might argue that he had the right to do so because his life would no longer be threatened. He was innocent in every way. Anointed to be king from a young age, he could have expedited his kingly appointment by removing King Saul. We read in verse 4 how David's men encouraged him to kill Saul in the cave. When we pause and meditate on what was taking place and the gravitas of the moment, we cannot miss what this portion of Scripture reveals to us. David was under severe pressure to follow the advice of his men, plus he had the golden opportunity to change his fortunes, save his life and better the future of the nation of Israel, or so it seemed.

David could have avenged Saul's attempts to kill him by killing Saul himself, but it would have angered God. It was not God's plan for David to prematurely become king over Israel in a self-promotional move. We can easily miss important messages in Scripture such as this moment.

David was in a position to kill Saul and in the mind of the untrained and inexperienced leader, it made good sense. He had the necessary training. However, instead of following his own mind, David resisted the enticement of a premature appointment. He ignored the voices of his inexperienced companions and obeyed the voice of his Shepherd. If David had killed Saul by taking the bait of the pseudo-promotion into a premature appointment as king, he would have gone against God's anointed king by obeying his men and disobeying God. Killing Saul would have brought condemnation on himself and the nation of Israel. Up to that point, David had enjoyed the blessings of God, but killing Saul would have unleashed the punishment of God on his life.

How David's story fits in with true faith

There's an interesting similarity with Jesus being tried by the religious leaders and Roman rulers. He did not act against them, but allowed His Father to judge them. David's test in the Cave of

Adullam shows us a link between the believer's life of faith and how the enemy always tries to derail such a trust in God. We see that before any great release or victory in the life of a believer, there's always a fake push towards a self-centred or a self-promoted achievement. It always begins with a temptation to "do it yourself". This temptation is designed to cause a fall just before the great event God had planned takes place. The enemy is watching the believer to see where their weaknesses are. He will exploit these for his own benefit. He will mask the opportunity as a promotion to convince the believer of its authenticity. He is the master of deception and markets the fake opportunity as if it is the perfect timing God has created for them. For the non-discerning believer, it can seem like the hand of God and they won't question the offer. If the person can discern and look beyond the opportunity, the merits and logic of the offer will become evident. Should the believer be able to wait upon God to clarify if this is His will for their life, the origin of the offer would become clear. The difference at the start might seem insignificant, but the greater the distance from the origin, the greater the fault. Mistakenly taking the premature offer or misreading the hand from which it comes, could spell disaster for the person and those around them.

Derailing a faith journey

The same principle applies to a person locked in a journey during a faith battle. Such a journey always comes with a fake premature event to derail the person waiting for God's answer to their prayer request. It's during such a time when the person's discernment and experience will be tested and it's crucial that the person learns to walk in sensitivity to everything that takes places in and around them.

Things can get challenging during a faith journey. Often the believer might be under such pressure that giving up, surrendering or walking away seems like an answer to prayer. The enemy is a crafty strategist and often, after experiencing setbacks, delays and suffering, "another option" appears. To the inexperienced believer, this is God's hand, when in fact, it is a plan by the enemy to derail their faith progress and in most cases, this so-called other option is a sugar-coated sinful deed. One of the greatest enemies of faith is sin, because faith is trust and trust is eroded by sin.

Any relationship is built on the premise of trust and when trust is broken, so is the relationship. Our relationship with God is built on faith, which is expressed in our obedience to His will and His Word. The level of our obedience to God's Word can be seen as a sign of our commitment to the relationship He offers us. Every believer needs to know that the enemy is jealous of this eternal relationship God offers the believer and he'd do everything in his power to derail it.

There is a moment just before a faith request is fulfilled or granted by God to the believer, and it's in this moment, some call it a deciding window of opportunity, when the enemy launches his attack. What looks like a genuine offer coming to the believer is in fact a temptation to derail the believer. It closely resembles David's opportunity in the cave to kill Saul and expedite his appointment as king over Israel. Taking it will undo everything the believer has worked for and postpone God's work in their lives. Such an offer is often subtle yet destructive, and will do serious damage to the relationship they have with God.

A believer who aims for great faith victories early on will be deceived into taking a fake offer to gain an early fleshly promotion. Normally, these early victories come easy and the believer doesn't have to work hard to achieve them. No patience is required and no sacrifice is necessary. These are some of the signs to look out for when walking by faith and patiently holding on for God's answer in times of delay. Pressure, delays and impulsivity often cause people to act without discernment. It blinds them into thinking that the first hand that's extended to them is the hand of God. I dare to say that in most cases the first hand is not the hand of God. It's a hand offering a promotion to the flesh and it is likely to circumvent costly spiritual growth and pruning towards spiritual development. This first hand offered during a delay will in most cases pander to the person's fleshly desires, which confirms that no spiritual growth has taken place. To discern which hand is God's, the flesh must first be moved aside. Spiritual growth is eternal, and ignorantly grasping at a premature offer will liquidate a believer's eternal rewards. The stakes are just too high to live in ignorance.

Chapter 10

Transitioning into something new

There are phases in the life of every person that need to be approached with wisdom. Although the context, history or personality of every person might differ, the principle stays the same. We must all manage several transitions in life, such as going from primary to high school; being a former prison inmate who's released; going from being single to married; parenthood; going through a divorce or the death of a loved-one, and so forth. A transition is a time of risk and uncertainty and is best managed by ensuring a sense of focus and making sure that a definite end goal is in sight. What comes with any transition is the risk of something being forgotten or left out in the process.

In Romans 1:16,17 Paul addresses faith. He starts with how an unbeliever is justified and then how they are to walk. Paul says that both justification and the journey of the believer are by faith. The conversion of the unbeliever into a believer and the journey towards spiritual maturity are both done by learning how to trust God. This process is called a transition because, before salvation takes place, the person is self-informed, self-governed and self-reliant. Everything pre-justification is done in the person's own wisdom, will and determination and apart from God. In their ignorance, they don't know what they're missing out on. Humanity was not created to depend on themselves for what they need.

To transition from being self-regulated to a believer who trusts God is a big move, and it doesn't happen automatically. It requires a planned approach to transition from self-leadership to being fully dependent on God. The believer needs to see that trusting God works; that placing hope in Scripture and waiting for God to honour His Word is an amazing process. Once the believer is convinced that Scripture is alive and working, they will be willing to place more and more reliance on God's Word. Initially this will be limited to significant events during difficult times, but then they will begin employing faith in their daily lives and decisions by yielding to the voice of the Spirit of God. Initially the voice of self-reliance is dominant, but as the believer tests and confirms for themself that God honours His Word, the reliance on the Spirit's voice will increase. We know that the Spirit and the Word are always in agreement, and once the believer has tasted God's faithfulness, this will lead to an increased sensitivity to the Spirit's leading. This transition takes time while trust in God is built.

A crucial aspect during this time of building trust in God is to shift reliance from self to God, which requires a step-by-step moving away from making their own decisions to having a high Word knowledge in their hearts and minds. The reliance on God is stepping away from their emotions. God's Word settles the believer with the knowledge that someone much bigger, wiser, more powerful and all-knowing is in charge of their life. For believers to transition away from relying on themselves is to do what God intended from the beginning; it's a progressive process and not a once-off event.

Reckless faith

Earlier I discussed blind hope relating to the claim that something will take place even though the person has no objective reality or truth to back up their claim. A classic example of this is the believer who claim the numbers of the Lotto will be given to them and that God will bless them to become wealthy through this. This is subjective speculation and, in most cases, has no Biblical foundation. Believers use the John 4:14 to claim that we can ask Jesus for anything and He will do it. That is what Jesus said in verse 14, but proper exegesis shows that there are several conditions that must first be met before we can truthfully stand before God and make our requests known to Him.

I would describe blind faith as someone who walks in Scriptural ignorance because they don't know the Word of God. Jesus said in John 9:41 that such a blindness will not be seen as a sin, however, the person will not receive what they're asking for because of their selfish requests. If we look at one of the conditions Jesus set in John 14:13,14, which is a litmus test, we see that God must be glorified in what we ask for. A person operating in blind faith is like a person born blind who has a guide dog. They're kept safe from pitfalls and dangerous obstacles, but they're unable to exercise their own authority and walk by themselves.

Another path people use when it comes to faith is embarking on reckless activities. Reckless faith falls into the category of believers performing acts that are out of the ordinary. I recently heard of a South African pastor who told his congregation that those who had fallen behind in their tithes should sell their homes and bring the money to the church. Unfortunately, there would be believers who have no sense of wisdom and would do such a thing. Other believers make life-threatening choices, such as the pastor from Mozambique who, in February 2023, went on a forty-day fast as Jesus did, and died on the twenty-fifth day.

What we see in these activities performed by believers in the name of faith is that if God had not called them to it, it's bound to end in disaster. A good example is when Peter climbed out of the boat and walked on water. The difference between what Peter did and what other believers do is that Jesus called Peter to walk on the water (Matthew 14:20) which was witnessed by others. Before a believer commits to a radical activity such as Peter's there should first be a verifiable call from Jesus for them to do so. Jesus invited people to show their faith in him by bringing Him their needs and the Bible recounts faith activities that often defied general rules. For instance the unclean woman who touched Jesus; Peter stepping out of the boat to walk on water; the four friends who lowered their sick friend through a roof so he could reach Jesus; David standing up to Goliath; and many more.

Deuteronomy 1:42 shows what happened to the Israelites when people acted without the invitation from God.

> But the Lord said to [Moses], "Tell them, 'Do not go up and fight, because I will not be with you. You will be defeated by your enemies.'"

What we need to understand

In Scripture we learn that God's plan of salvation is to reconcile us to Himself, which He does by giving His Son as a sacrificial lamb to atone for sin. Our entrance into this plan is with the gift of faith, given by the Spirit of God. However, this is not the only gift we receive. The Spirit of God gives us the gift of life and a desire to follow God. As we develop in our walk with God, we increasingly display the attributes of Jesus.

False teachers erroneously claim that faith is the "tool" to get what you want. Faith is given to us by God and His Spirit is at work in us to sanctify us. This means He's washing away the old sinful nature and replacing it with the nature of Christ. Focusing on faith alone is a grave mistake. We've not only received the gift of faith, but also the Spirit who's forming the Person of Christ within us. How can we see this? We see this as the fruit of the Spirit becomes evident in our thoughts and actions.

> But the fruit of the Spirit is love, joy, peace, patience, kind-
> ness, goodness, faithfulness, gentleness, and self-control.
> Against such things there is no law. Galatians
> 5:22,23 (NET)

When faith is taught as a tool to receive what we desire, we focus on personal desires only. It causes people to overlook what God desires for every believer, which is a Godly character developed over time. Faith must lead to a life of obedience to God's commands. The role of the Spirit is to give birth to the life of God within a believer and to achieve spiritual maturity within the believer. What faith-based teachings have done is to focus solely on achieving the next best thing, invoking the desires of the flesh and not God's.

This may promote living by faith, but it ignores the fruits of the Spirit such as patience and self-control. Faith is not a tool given to us by God to rebuild what Jesus came to tear down. Jesus came to bring an end to the desires of the flesh and His death on the cross made it possible for us to die to the old carnal way of living. The Spirit plays a pivotal role in all the aspects of our spiritual birth, development and maturity. Yes, He gives us spiritual gifts to achieve what people cannot achieve by themselves, but we must not focus solely on the one gift and ignore the other functions of the Spirit in the life of the believer.

The enemy's aim

Earlier I explained how faith is used interchangeably with trust. The life of a believer is a journey of learning to trust God. Trust functions within the confines of a relationship where mutual trust exists, and in this relationship, God cannot lie, deceive or change His Word. We can place our total trust in Him.

Why does the enemy pursue the trust the believer has in God? Satan is extremely jealous of the relationship the believer has with God, which can be seen in Genesis 3:1-5 (Adam and Eve), in Matthew 4:1-11 (the temptation of Jesus), and in Deuteronomy 1:32 and Hebrews 4. His aim is to drive a wedge between the believer and God. Once he dismantles the relationship, trust is lost and faith cannot function. The relationship between God and the believer begins with faith and is built on faith, which sustains the believer and connects them to God. If trust in the relationship is broken, the bridge that carries spiritual blessings from God to the believer is removed.

The enemy's poisonous darts have not changed since he attacked Adam and Eve in Genesis 3:1-5. He subtly questions God's Word and the believer's knowledge of the Word to see if he could get the believer to doubt what God has said. His next step is to counter or replace God's Word. He's very systematic in his approach with the single aim of eroding the believer's trust in God. When he can question God's Word and get the believer to doubt God's Word, he has succeeded in being a third party to the relationship. He will lie, deceive and sow seeds of doubt to get the believer to look to themself for all they need. People are totally dependent on God for every breath they take and their pursuit to be independent of God is doomed from the start.

Chapter 11

Yoked to this world

In this book, the reader will find an important aspect highlighted many times – that faith is a gift to accomplish what we as believers, or people in general, cannot accomplish in our own strength. No matter how advanced humanity has and will become, they cannot reach into the realm of the Spirit. This world is as real to us as the tangible things we see, however, Scripture explains in Genesis 1:2 that the realm of the Spirit existed before the natural world.

Faith is the vehicle that allows an unbeliever to be justified by God. Scripture does not provide any other method by which a person can be saved eternally and it specifically precludes people's works to achieve salvation. This is an important aspect because being justified is not the beginning and the end of salvation; it's just the first step towards an eternal relationship with God. In Romans 1:17, when Paul says that the righteous shall live by faith, he's not referring to being justified; he's talking post-justification in this verse. It speaks of a continuous revelation to the believer regarding the righteousness of God and is not a quick once-off. Paul is saying that the justified person will progressively see that the way the believer was saved by grace through faith (Ephesians 2:8,9) will be the way they will live. The outworking of this verse is that the believer will depend on God for their justification and for every day and everything needed thereafter. It's a new lifestyle the believer must begin to walk in and it's an awareness of what God expects from the believer that needs to take root in the heart of the justified person.

Faith is an "emptying of oneself". It's also a gift that accomplishes in the Spirit what cannot be accomplished in the flesh and, for this reason, faith exercised by a believer pleases God (Hebrews 11:6). When faith accomplishes what a person cannot do in their own wisdom and strength, then what is accomplished takes on a whole new meaning.

If God was pleased with what we can accomplish in our own strength and wisdom, we wouldn't need faith. Jesus came to set us free from sin (Matthew 1:21) and to do this we need to exercise our gift of faith. Thereafter begins a new journey for the believer. God expects us to walk free from sin and its entanglements in our lives.

How do we do this? Well, I'm glad you asked. We begin by being justified first and thereafter we begin to put a distance between us and this world. God did not call us to leave this world after we have been justified. No, He expects us to master this world and all it is, says, offers and demands. Faith serves to empower us to walk free from this world's enticing offers, its temptations and its smokescreens. Behind what this world offers is despair, death and destruction. We first need to be justified and second, sanctified, which is where the Word of God and our understanding of it wash us from the filth found in this world. Sin has corrupted this world and entanglement with this world means our devotion to God is stained.

What Romans 1:17 says is that should the believer not walk by faith, they will not be able to withstand the cleverly designed schemes this world offers. Remember that faith is not a tool for the believer to accomplish earthly feats; faith is gifted to us to accomplish what the Spirit desires in us. When a person walks in true faith, they exemplify a believer who's not unequally yoked with this world (2 Corinthians 6:14-16 and John 17:16). Faith empowers believers to see the often disguised lies and deceit offered by the world and it creates a need for the believer to cry to God for help to be free from the sinful world. Jesus was clear when He said that an investment in this world is foolish; it rusts, weathers and gets stolen. His advice to believers is investment in what has eternal value (Matthew 6:19-21).

Believers who distort faith to increase their worldly treasures have been deceived. To walk by faith is to employ faith to please God and not to yoke ourselves to this world. Faith empowers the believer to resist the temptations of this world, which believers cannot accomplish in their own strength and wisdom. Making this world our lifetime investment is contrary to the words of both Jesus and the Apostle James (James 4:4). This doesn't mean we're not to do business in this world and make a living. What Scripture does preclude is investing all our time, energy and resources in this world, which is idolatry.

To be void of faith removes the unique aspect that believers have, which is to be distinguishable from this world and the temporary rewards it offers. An absence of faith in the life of a believer will see them busy themselves with the things of this world with no time for the things of God.

How faith reveals sin

We've established that faith enables us to do what we cannot do for ourselves. We also know that faith is a way of trusting God for His protection, provision and guidance. Faith bridges the gap between where we are at the point of being unsaved to where we are saved and become Christians. Faith is putting our trust in God to receive material and spiritual things we cannot naturally receive; it's a spiritual force that enables us to live in the spirit.

Faith shows us that only God can achieve in us what He desires for us and we know from Scripture that we need to trust God for our entire spiritual life, from infancy to maturity. We need faith in our justification, during our process of sanctification and to finally reach our glorification. All three of these, which encompass the believer's entire spiritual life, are totally impossible in our own strength and wisdom. Faith means to lay down our efforts to be a better person and look to God for His power to both save and transform us on the inside.

Salvation cannot be achieved though human effort because of the presence of sin. Faith is the bridge that connects the unsaved person to God; it opens the door of grace to allow the Spirit of God into the heart of the unbeliever. No one can be saved by works (Isaiah 64:6 and Ephesians 2:9). Faith comes from hearing God's Word when salvation is preached (Romans 10:17) and it enables the unbeliever to reach out to God for salvation. From that moment on, faith plays a major role in the life of the believer.

At the start of the book we find the account of Israel's journey from Egyptian slavery, their journey through the Wilderness and their inheriting of the Promised Land, which was a walk of faith from beginning to end. But most of the Israelites who were part of the exodus never made it to the Promised Land. Hebrews 3 gives a clear reason why most of them perished in the desert – their downfall was their lack of faith in God, and Hebrews 3:12 places unbelief and sin in the same sentence.

Israel began a journey of self-righteousness and they argued that they didn't need God. This led to the hardening of their hearts, which in turn led to rebellion (Hebrews 3:8). Whenever people depend on their own strength to accomplish a spiritual goal, they will fail every time. We see this when Israel, against Moses' advice, sent their fighting men into battle. God warned them that He would not be with them and the result was great losses at the hands of their enemy (Deuteronomy 1:42).

Hebrews 3:12,13 speaks about unbelief as sin and that the deceitfulness of sin causes a person to turn away from God, which goes back to the event in the Garden of Eden where Adam believed the devil's lie and sought a better position for himself. 'You can be like God,' the devil said to Adam and Eve (Genesis 3:5), insinuating that they didn't need God and could continue autonomously into the future. Humanity was never created to be independent from God, but to be in an intimate relationship with Him, trusting God to provide for their needs, and to protect and guide them.

Many years later, the Israelites had the same mindset as Adam and Eve. They did not want God as their King, their provider nor their protector. They wanted to be self-governed, which was not what God planned for the nation He called His bride.

It's impossible for a person to please God because it's impossible for any human who is apart from Jesus to live a sin-free life. Humanity's sinful nature from birth has assured this (Psalm 51:5). Romans 1:5 says that obedience comes from faith. Faith is needed to rid a person of sin, because though the obedience it develops in the believer's heart, it expels the sin of disobedience.

A blameless walk

We can all emulate the faith of Abraham, called the father of our faith (Romans 4:12). In the New Testament where Abraham is mentioned, we read about him as the pioneer of faith in God; he was a friend of God and conversed with Him, which is something few other humans have had the privilege to do.

The Old Testament gives us details of crucial events that took place in Abraham's life when he met God. After his initial meeting with God in Genesis 12:1-3, God promised Abraham that he would have offspring. Abraham believed God and this was credited to him as righteousness (Genesis 15:6).

In chapter 16, Abraham tried to bring to fruition what God had promised in his own way and he had a son with Hagar, thinking he had assisted God to fulfil the promise. This was a mistake that God called him out on. In Genesis 17:1 God speaks with Abram before his name was changed and gave him a command that must not be overlooked. God says, 'I am God Almighty; walk before me faithfully and be blameless.' God required a blameless walk from Abraham who couldn't hide anything from God. Abraham became the father of many nations, the receiver of God's promises and the example of faith to us all by meeting God's condition.

Imagine you're a fisherman who grew up fishing daily in the family business. You've learnt to judge the direction and strength of the wind, the motion of the waves, the seasons and so forth. You're well-trained and you know the fishing business. Then one day you're asked to get into your boat and cross to the other side. A terrible storm hits your boat out of nowhere. All your training, experience and skills are rendered worthless in an instant and you've nowhere to run. Then you realise that the very person who created the earth, the universe, the wind and the waves is asleep in your boat and you go to Jesus and wake Him up. His first words are: 'Where is your faith?' (Luke 8:22-25).

Jesus' question to His disciples was not to determine the location of their faith. This is similar to the question God asked Adam after the fall into sin (Genesis 3:8). God knew Adam's physical location; He wanted Adam to express the state of his heart after his fall. Jesus' question to his disciples was of a similar nature. It was a rhetorical question. He wanted them to see that their hope to survive the storm had been rooted in themselves – in their years of experience in the fishing business on Lake Galilee. Jesus wanted them to understand that their faith during the storm was in their own strength and experience, not in Him, the foundation of faith.

My personal faith journey

During a recent faith project, I felt as if someone was choking me amid all the tests, it felt as if I was in a perfect storm. This was not a faith project I had put my hand up for; it had become a project of economic survival. I was beginning to ask God to take this burden away from me. I was overwhelmed and what made things worse were other problems that flooded my life. I was starting to become angry. Why God; why me? Why do You allow this? Why do I have to experience multiple tests like this? I felt like Jacob who wrestled with God. I wanted an end to my struggle and to experience a time of freedom from all these battles.

While standing in church one Sunday morning, I felt weary because of the burden in my mind. There was nowhere to go to escape how I was feeling. This was the sort of pressure that influences your health, your sleep and your relationship with those around you. While standing in church, I said to myself: 'My flesh hates the whole process of faith.' Later in the day I experienced moments of weakness where my eyes drifted away from Jesus my Rock and the moment this happened, I felt a surge of hopelessness and despair.

What made this situation particularly difficult was that I could not pick up the phone and force someone to do their job. Everything was out of my control and, because of this, my flesh began to rebel. My mind was telling me to do the exact opposite of Scripture. I felt I had to take care of the situation myself; I didn't feel as if I could wait any longer. While studying the book of Hebrews, I came to a verse that spoke profoundly into my situation. Hebrews 3:8 says the Israelites did not trust God. The trials they experienced in the Wilderness coupled with a lack of faith in God, made their hearts turn against Him. Scripture calls this rebellion, which attracts God's harshest punishment (Hebrews 4:11).

My learnings

The harshest punishment a father can exert on his son is to break fellowship, to turn his face away; to banish the son from His presence. In a sense, it's a picture of what the eternal separation between believers and non-believers will look like. Why would

God mete out such a harsh penalty on a person? It's clear from the book of Hebrews that trust is an important aspect to God; it is developed over time but can be undone in a moment of distrust. God's harshest punishment is applied to those who break trust with Him – even those who once walked close to Him (Numbers 20:12).

The Old Testament tells how Israel tested God in the Wilderness. He supplied their every need; He did miracle after miracle and made His dwelling among them. He displayed His goodness to enable them to trust Him. What more could God have done for them? Despite all this, Israel doubted God when they faced challenges. In effect, it was like a son saying that he doesn't believe that his father can supply his needs, which is a violation of trust.

A similar event is recorded in the Luke 15 parable of the Prodigal Son. The son demanded his portion of the father's estate even though his father was still alive, showing that he regarded his father as good as dead – a disrespectful and distrustful act against a loving father.

In John 10:38 Jesus told the crowds that if they did not believe in the words He spoke, they should believe in Him because of the miracles He performed. He was saying that despite all the miracles He performed, they still did not believe in Him. This was the exact history of Israel. No matter how many times God performed miracles and demonstrated His power, Israel still refused to trust Him. They murmured and rebelled and even rejected God as their King (1 Samuel 8:7). We see from both the Old and New Testament that trusting God is not easy, yet for those able to achieve it, it brings a true and lasting benefit.

Hebrews 4: 10 refers to the rest a believer must enter. This rest represents handing over your decisions, your concerns and your future to God. By emptying yourself of wanting to make it work yourself, you enter God's rest. It's when a believer abandons their own fleshly efforts and allows God to take over. Israel failed greatly in this area. They had a fair-weather relationship with God and wanted to dictate to both Him and Moses what they wanted. When He supplied their needs, they rejoiced, but when challenges arrived, they rebelled against the One who saved them from slavery. They quickly turned to idols to do their bidding. The believer who allows God to guide their decisions, whether they agree with God's direction or not, is a believer who will enter God's rest. To hand over control of your destiny might be tough to do initially and it may make you feel vulnerable, but you'll see and experience God's faithfulness and over time you'll have no reservations about trusting God again and again.

My naughty corner

I put myself in the naughty corner of believers who get frustrated disappointed with God when we don't immediately see a break-through in our situation. In my case, as pressure mounted and an answer was seemingly not forthcoming, I became frustrated with the situation. To be honest, I was frustrated with God Himself. If He was the One who has the power to change my situation, then He was the One withholding the answer. During times of intense prayer, I became persuaded that I was confusing the object and the author of my faith. I remained content when the answer seemed imminent, but when it lingered, I become frustrated. This was because of weak Bible interpretation principles on my side.

Because of the pressure brought on by the circumstances, I erro-neously placed my hope in the object of my faith and not in the author of my faith (Hebrews 12:2). I quoted Hebrews 11:1 and claimed that faith was the assurance of the object I hoped to receive. I placed my trust in the outcome of my hope, namely on receiving my answer, and not in the person who authors and completes my faith – the One who provides the answer. Then I began to realise that the more I used my faith, the deeper my relationship with Jesus grew.

When we anchor our trust in the person of Jesus, the author and finisher of our faith, we entrust our requests to Him. He is our joy, our fulfilment, our sustainer and provider. The moment we do this, our rest begins (Hebrews 4:10). Rest means we lay down our work and He begins to work on our behalf to fulfil our needs. His wisdom will also protect us against ourselves when our requests are fleshly in nature. When it is a real worldly need, He will answer and provide it. This way we entrust our request to Him and we begin to rest in His wisdom and provision.

Always remember that when our joyous expectation is anchored in the outcome of our request, we will never be able to enter His rest. We will strive and work until we receive or obtain what our flesh wants.

Seeing is not believing

Jesus said to Thomas that seeing is not believing. He also said that those who maintain their trust in Him, despite not seeing the results yet, are blessed (John 20:29). Jesus was giving an open and personal invitation to His disciples to put Him first and not what they could see.

Thomas's remarks showed distrust and Jesus made it clear to him that he would not receive any blessing. Thomas put his personal preferences ahead of Jesus' teachings. Like many of us, Thomas wanted his flesh to be satisfied. Jesus highlighted the battle within Thomas, which was the fight between Thomas's flesh and his spirit – trusting what's easy and visible and can be understood.

The account of Jesus calming the storm is another example of how the flesh is at war with the Spirit. The disciples were caught in a deadly storm at sea and after trying everything they summoned Jesus to save them. Jesus did the impossible in front of their eyes, and while some began understanding His true marvellous identity, some still doubted (Matthew 28:17). Even seeing the wonders Jesus performed could not convince some of His disciples to put their trust in Him, which shows that trusting God is a personal decision every person must take. This decision will initiate a war between the mind and the spirit of a person.

Those who live by faith are special people who live life differently to the rest of the world. They're not driven by the spirit of this age, by a desire to prove themselves, by a lust for wealth or worldly profit. They're a people who live in this world with their eyes set on the life to come. They're a people who have, as Paul said in 2 Timothy 4:7,8, won the fight between the flesh (the mind) and the work of the Spirit. They've honoured God more than anything else and have overcome this world.

Chapter 12

The Lord of my will

The word "Lord" is used close on 7,000 times in Scripture. It depicts the position of a master over a person. Calling someone Lord means you have submitted your will to your master's. However, saying you submit and actually doing it could be worlds apart.

The power of the human will is incredibly strong. It can resist and overcome incredible threats and it can be a great asset, but it can also be a hindrance. Paul instructs us to walk by faith, which demands a surrender of our will. This does not mean a believer has to ignore or set aside the natural talents and gifts God has given them, but these abilities and gifts are earthbound and cannot affect or alter things in the spirit realm. The flesh cannot change or dictate to the spirit. God has destined the flesh to be powerless to change things in the spirit. It's the spirit who dictates to and affects the flesh.

When we speak of submitting to God as our Master, it means we are to allow the Spirit of God to direct our ways. When we do this, He begins to employ the natural talents and gifts He gave us to serve God and bring glory to His name. If this step of submission doesn't take place, there will be a war between the person's flesh and the Spirit of God. Even though the flesh uses its natural thinking and abilities, it still walks totally blind in the spirit realm (John 3:6; Romans 8:3-10). When a person's mind is not renewed, it is not submitted to God, which means it will want to dictate to the Spirit what should happen in the realm of the spirit.

Since the creation, people have relied on their own decision-making abilities to express their inner will. This is humanity's default nature and to deny themselves and submit to God's will is easier said than done. God uses many ways to bring people to Himself. He allows them to come to a halt so that they can evaluate who they are and who He is. God often uses a series of events that He allows to get the believer's attention. He will never force Himself on someone, but He will do all He can to get the person to experience a life of freedom, a life lived in submission to His will. The believer might be unwilling to surrender their will to the Master's, predominantly because they've never experienced God's supernatural provision in their lives. Relinquishing control is not an easy step, but once the believer experiences the benefit of doing so, allowing God to lead becomes their default nature.

Scripture shows us that people are drawn to an environment where they're acknowledged, appreciated and valued. It also shows us that a person who stands up for their faith will immediately have a target on their back. Paul made this clear when he spoke about the revelation he had and how he walked by faith. If you stand up for believing in God you become "public enemy number one". Wherever you go, it seems as if you're being followed by an adversary.

Scripture teaches us that the enemy is out to destroy those who trust in God, but he's not the only one pursuing them. God pursues the believer, not to destroy them, but to deliver and purify them. His motive is diametrically opposed to the enemy's. The hand of God often touches the life of a believer and its effects can be lifelong, such as the encounter Jacob had with God (Genesis 32:25). His hand begins to work in the life of the believer to remove anything that's of the flesh. Eternal life is too precious to take unnecessary risks.

First, God is willing to offend a believer and even touch their physical bodies to get His message of eternity through to them. Second, God will not allow the flesh to boast because faith is a gift from God and it serves to glorify God not people. Ephesians 2:9 says that faith works apart from a person's efforts so that no one can boast when it comes to the achievements of faith.

There appears to be a common thread between the level of revelation and the level of severity God allows a believer's flesh to be touched. His aim is to strip off and cut away anything in the believer that could allow the flesh to boast. Something done without trusting God will cause a person's flesh to demand acknowledgement and glory. When faith achieves its goal in the life of the believer, God is always glorified, but when the flesh sets out to achieve something, the glory is taken from God. No person or created being is worthy of receiving any glory.

Jesus gave His life so that the pursuits and achievements of the flesh may be brought to nothing. The greater the calling on a person's life, the greater the person's dependence should be on God for guidance and wisdom. I am saying it "should" be on God, because sometimes people taste the glory and they want more and begin to take the glory for themselves. It's at this point that the hand of God is set in motion and He begins to dismantle whatever the believer is building. Sometimes, in the extreme, the person might even lose their life, but live eternally (1 Corinthians 5:5).

The lives of the apostles Paul, John and Peter all speak of incredible revelations they received from God and how they suffered for it. We should not misunderstand their sufferings because what they lost on earth was for the sake of gaining an eternal reward in the life to come. Did God allow their sufferings? Indeed He did, because this life is a place of transition into the eternal home awaiting every believer. God's hand was active in all of their lives to accomplish His will.

Often believers begin a walk by faith, but later abandon it. This tends to happen because of the intimidation and struggles that go hand-in-hand with walking by faith. Jesus made it clear in Mark 4:17 that trouble and persecution come for one reason only – to oppose the Word of God that the person has received. Once a person has tasted faith that accompanies the Word of God (Romans 10:17), they become unstoppable. For this reason the enemy will do anything in his power to oppose the Word as early in the process as possible.

The struggles and persecutions that many believers experience are there to develop and purify those who walk by faith. God allows them, as we see in the account of Job's life. God uses them to test a person's heart, to purify, develop and validate their faith. The person realises that to achieve what God has called them to can only be accomplished by faith, and this purifies the believer's convictions. The believer's faith is developed once they've passed through a difficult season and can testify that only by God's grace did they make it through. In this way the difficulties associated with faith develop them. Lastly, when faith has run its full course in someone's life, they've proven that God's Word is faithful; they've withstood the test of faith and received their reward or blessing as promised in Hebrews 11:6. This way the person is validated before God.

The mature believer will understand and recognise the hand of God during a journey of development; they will acknowledge what God is doing and why. The believer who has placed their trust in God understands their Father's input in their lives and the need for it. To an immature believer, the journey of faith can be a challenging time and it can feel as if God is against them. This is especially true when God is pruning their hearts. Believers often question, misunderstand or even blame God's work on an attack by the enemy. Why would the God of love allow or cause suffering in their lives? Surely He does not condone pain, suffering and persecution in the life of a believer? I urge the reader to read the accounts of the apostles in Scripture to see the effects of true faith and how it affected those who placed their total trust in God.

What we learn from Old Testament battles

Israel's journey out of 400 years of Egyptian slavery into the Wilderness and to the Promised Land is a theme in the Old Testament that contains myriad lessons for us as believers. We can see what God expected from them; we see their highs and lows, their victories and their failures – and what stands out is how they had to learn to trust God. From escaping the clutches of Pharaoh through the lamb's blood on the doorposts, to walking through the desolate Sinai desert and fighting to enter and inherit the Promised Land.

In the Old Testament this journey is expressed as a journey of trusting God (Deuteronomy 8:2). For us today, we're taught to put our faith in God (Hebrews 11:1). The multiplex theme of Egypt, Wilderness and Promised Land is again seen in the New Testament in the form of justification, which means freedom from sin slavery; sanctification, which details the believer's washing away of sin by the Spirit of God using the Word of God; and glorification, which refers to the ultimate fulfilling of God's plan where all believers reside with God eternally.

Many of Israel's battles are described in the Old Testament and their toughest phase was the forty years in the Wilderness. During this time Israel was stripped of anything and everything they had in Egypt and they had to depend on God for their provision and protection. The Wilderness didn't offer them food, water or protection from the elements and they were greatly challenged (Deuteronomy 8:2). God planned this time to humble them and test their obedience to His commands. They had to be transformed in their minds from trusting in idols and providing for themselves from the Egyptian supplies to totally relying on God for everything they needed.

In the Promised Land Israel had to contend with the Amorites, Philistines, Amalekites and many other nations. They needed to fight these nations to inherit the Promised Land. However, Hebrews reveals that Israel's greatest battle was not against pagan nations; it was the challenge to overcome their lack of trust in God (Numbers 14:11; Hebrews 4:2).

We know that trusting God is also expressed as believing in God, which relates to obedience to God. What could have been the greatest gift became the greatest loss. The promise of their own land where they would live with God dwelling among them became a Wilderness where the distrusting Israelites died and were buried in the desert. Few of the adults who left Egypt did not enter the Promised Land. And many of those who did enter were later driven out of the land into exile again – for the same reasons: unbelief and rebellion. Their distrust made God their enemy and He showed His dismay by dealing with it harshly. The process of Israel's rebellion and punishment is a mirror image of Adam and Eve's treason against God and their expulsion from the Garden of Eden.

Today, the believer's greatest challenge is to set aside their own ideas, desires and will. Within the heart of every believer is a person who wants to go their own way and fight their own battles. God's plan of salvation is not to strengthen the believer's will and personal desires, but to end the rebellion and start a new life in the Spirit – to walk in step with the Spirit as the Old Testament Israelites needed to walk in step with God's commands, His will and His ways.

When rebirth takes place in a believer (John 3:3), it's not natural for them to just let go and hand over control of their mind, their lives and their decision-making to God. Immediately after being born again, an epic battle begins within the heart of the new believer (Deuteronomy 8:2) and they're called to surrender to God. Let's be honest – human beings like being in charge. The battle in the heart of every believer is greater than any external challenge they will face and it rages for the rest of their lives on earth (Romans 12:2).

We live in a world where we're encouraged to be our own destiny makers. The world out there says that success or failure are in our own grasp, and that through hard work and personal improve-ment, we can reach the top of the proverbial ladder. Society spends time, resources and effort chasing impossible solutions. But what people are after – the peace and security they so desire – are outside their ability to accomplish. God doesn't save someone so that they can embark on a journey of improving themselves; He saves them to totally transform them. He does this by exposing them to the challenges faced by every person daily. Similar to the Israelites' Wilderness journey, the challenges that believers face are meant expose their hearts and their willingness to change. The obedience that comes from faith is what God looks for.

Chapter 13

The role of the Father

F aith is a gift from our Father in heaven; it's like a bridge that allows us to approach Him for salvation and for our earthly needs. Hebrews 11:6 says that faith is a method or a bridge we are given to reach out to God. We can get God's attention by using this bridge; it's the only way we can transition from our mortal boundary into the spiritual world where God exists. Ephesians 2:8,9 says salvation is by grace through faith alone, which means that believers can change their eternal destiny from death to life by trusting God. By accessing this spiritual gift of faith, people can receive justification by God and be assured of eternity in heaven and not in hell.

Faith is a gift from the Father and when we use this gift it's important that we understand where it came from and what its purpose is. The Father plays a three-fold role in our understanding of the spiritual gift of faith. First, He makes the spiritual gift of faith available to the unbeliever to receive justification. Second, the Father responds to the believer when they approach Him by faith to receive things they need and cannot do or achieve in their own wisdom and strength. Third, the Father uses the process of faith to develop deep trust in the believer though various steps. It's a process in which the flesh – the carnal nature – must be crucified and put to death. Up the point of salvation, people rely on themselves and use their own judgement. To live by faith, the believer needs more than a mere makeover. Their whole being must be reborn to trust God. If not, they'll return to what they previously depended on throughout their life.

God created Adam and gave him work to do in the Garden of Eden to rule over all creatures. Before Adam sinned, faith was not needed by people. It was only after Adam and Eve sinned and lost the glory of God that people needed a mechanism to return to God. The Father was gracious in giving humanity the spiritual gift of faith to enable them to respond to His reconciliation initiative. When we read about Peter walking on water, we see that when he began to sink, Jesus extended a hand to rescue him (Matthew 14:31). It's this extended hand that best depicts God's view of humanity and the faith mechanism He's made available to them.

During Adam's time in the garden, his obedience to God's commands was key. Immediately after they sinned, faith was needed to reach out to God to be reunited with their creator. In Jesus' final hour on the cross, we see the same principle in how He cries out to His Father (Matthew 27:46). This shows us the role of the Father who never rejects anyone who cries out to Him for help.

Like a tree in an orchard

The Father also sustains those who belong to Him. Compare a tree in a forest to a fruit tree in a farmer's orchard – there's a big difference. The tree in the forest lives and when its lifespan is reached, it dies for any of a number of reasons – forest fire, human deforestation or age. Compare this to a tree in an orchard that's planted for a specific purpose and goes through various processes. From seedling stage, the trees get the personal attention of the farmer. They're cultivated in an orchard where they're given fertiliser and water and are monitored constantly because they're expected to add value to the orchard. This value is reflected in the owner farmer's joy.

Not only is planting seedlings a joyous day for the farmer but it's also a process he commits to and will complete (Hebrews 12:2). The farmer will ensure that each tree is inspected and pruned of any possible deformities regularly. In Isaiah 61:3, God refers to believers as 'oaks of righteousness'. Genesis also refers to trees God had planted – some had a general purpose and others had a very specific purpose – and God has an expectation for every tree. We are the trees in God's grove and it's the responsibility of every tree to find out from the "farmer" what their specific purpose is. Once we understand the purpose we've been planted for, we will begin to understand and appreciate the pruning processes we experience in the seasons of our lives.

Jesus said that a believer will be known by their fruit (Matthew 7:15-20) and in John 15:2 He said that pruning is a guarantee, not only as a sign of ownership, but also to ensure increased productivity. Nurturing every tree leads to increased productivity, which reflects the nature of the owner. Fruit trees are pruned for several reasons: trees will yield more fruit when their branches are trimmed; trees are trimmed into a shape that allows one main stem to grow upward to harness more water and sunlight; and the open shape enables enough airflow through the tree to prevent disease.

A tree's productivity is also stimulated by fertilising and feeding of the tree's soil, which ensures healthy growth and enables the tree to fight off diseases. Another aspect to note is that while all the trees undergo general treatment, the owner also gives special treatment to specific trees when needed.

Aspects of faith

Hebrews 11 is known as the faith hero chapter and Hebrews 12 continues with key aspects of faith that we need to understand.

> Therefore, since we are surrounded by such a great cloud of witnesses, let us throw off everything that hinders and the sin that so easily entangles. And let us run with perseverance the race marked out for us, fixing our eyes on Jesus, the pioneer and perfecter of faith. For the joy that was set before him he endured the cross, scorning its shame, and sat down at the right hand of the throne of God. Hebrews 12: 1,2 (NIV)

Most important to remember is that Jesus went before us and endured the sacrifice toward atonement for us all. He now sits with the Father and speaks on our behalf. Verses 5 to 17 address endurance. What endurance does it refer to? It refers to the role of the Father who either allows testing to mature us or disciplines and chastises us Himself.

But it's important also to view faith from the Father's perspective, which offers a new understanding of the workings of faith between a father and son, or between a tree and the orchard owner's expectations.

Unlike many false preachers who portray faith as something to use to 'get what I want', faith is not a way to fulfil the desires of the flesh. Faith always seeks to glorify God. If faith was a way to gratify the flesh, then God made a mistake in giving us this powerful spiritual gift. Faith, as said earlier, is God's way to restore us back to Himself – to reconcile every individual in the universe with their creator. Faith is what allows us to respond to God's loving sacrifice of His Son to be saved. Without faith, we could not reach out and receive the impossible; God's forgiveness and the restoration of the relationship with Him that we were created for.

By faith we are reborn to live lives that please God. By faith we worship the God who created us and who sent His Son to save us. By faith we look to the One who promised to keep us safe from the enemy's attacks and the One who provides everything we need. By faith we, as children of God, put our future in the hands of the all-knowing One who sees and knows the future. By faith we set aside the values we've grown up with and what we see around us. By faith we follow what the inspired Word of God shows us to be holy living. By faith we live in a world that goes to extreme efforts to argue away the existence of God.

In Hebrews 11:10-16 we read about people who lived by faith, who trusted God and only saw their reward in the next life. They held onto God in unwavering trust in His faithfulness to do what He had promised. Their hope was anchored in Him, even if what they asked for did not come true in this life.

Faith expressed as trust leads to an obedience to God's will and His ways. Obeying Him glorifies God and demonstrates eternal love, as Jesus said in John 14:15-17. Faith is a gift from the Spirit of God who builds a bridge to lead us into a pure life on earth and into eternity. No person can reach into the eternal spiritual world in their own wisdom and strength. It takes faith to hear the voice of God and respond to Him.

By understanding that faith is a spiritual gift from God to be used to glorify Him, we begin to set our eyes on the world to come and not so much on this world. Hebrews 11 details how the faith heroes looked for the eternal city of God, and we too should view our daily lives, our work ethic and relationships with the same mindset. Faith is there to assist us in our daily needs, not our fleshly wants, and to live the Great Commission Jesus has called us to. Faith is ours to change us to have the nature of Christ.

When we correctly employ faith as the spiritual gift that it is, the spiritual world and the things pertaining to God become a focal point in our lives and what the world around us offers looks increasingly pitiful and valueless. If we don't live by faith, the evidence will show that we continually invest more in this world and its fading beauty than in the spiritual world to come (Matthew 6:19-21). Faith helps us to see above the temporary things of this earth and into the mind of Christ and what He's busy planning for us in heaven. When faith takes hold of us, the Gospel begins to champion our lives and we become increasingly involved in Christlike living. Our lives are changed from sinful and selfish to holy. Our efforts and energies are spent on how we can proliferate the message of the Gospel into every tribe, nation and tongue around the world.

Walking by faith allows us to see through the façade this world has created and expose the lies we're sold by the enemy who uses his disciples to keep as many away from God as possible. Faith opens our eyes to the real world, the world of the spirit, which is hidden from every person not reborn by the Spirit by faith. Through faith, the Spirit empowers us to hear His voice and to understand what Scripture reveals to us about what is to come. By faith our tomorrow is secure because we're in the hands of the One who holds tomorrow. Faith also guarantees our eternity with God through Christ Jesus, who deposits in our hearts the Spirit of God who will be with us forever (John 14:16).

Chapter 14

The correct steps to take

Quite often our needs are beyond human abilities and we need God to take charge – in this situation we must remember that there are specific steps to follow when we are in need. People often don't get answers to their requests because they've not followed the correct process for requests to God as laid out in Scripture. Philippians 4:6 clearly states the steps for presenting our requests before God.

> Do not be anxious about anything, but in every situation,
> by prayer and petition, with thanksgiving, present your
> requests to God. Philippians 4:6 (NIV)

Paul says we're not to be anxious. As we know, anxiety can cause people to be irrational and make poor decisions. Paul goes on to say that we're to present our requests to God through prayer, petition and thanksgiving – and when we look at what Scripture says about true faith, there's a lot we can learn here.

Take the example of the widow and the jar of oil in 2 Kings 4:1-7. This real-life account will help us establish what steps we are to take to correctly activate and apply our faith. Here we see a widow desperate for help when she speaks of her husband's death and his trust in God. She appealed to the prophet Elisha for help in her predicament. Contextually and historically, appealing to the prophet of God under the Old Covenant was a direct appeal to God. Elisha asked the woman what she had in her house that could be put to use to help her? It's interesting to note that the woman's trust was first anchored in God by approaching the man of God for help. She demonstrated her desperation and placed her problem at God's feet. What happened next was the practical answer to her spiritual problem when Elisha asked her what she had to offer as part of the solution.

Why is it so important to first lay your problem at God's feet? Why not just take charge and fix it yourself, using your own experience, wisdom and creativity? Well, when we face challenges, it's our human nature to push through alone and, in the process, we tend to prefer to stay in control. True faith, as this book explains, is letting go of all control and allowing God to take charge. Furthermore, during testing times our emotions can interfere with our decision-making, leading to a different outcome than the one God intended. This is often the case when prolonged waiting for an answer can weigh heavily on a person's mind and they're tempted to bail out or do something foolish. Philippians 4:6 says we're to keep praying and petitioning God.

Notice that if the widow had come up with the jar of oil as a proposed solution to her problem and thereafter confirmed her trust in God, the outcome would have been different. Providing God with a solution to her problem and asking Him to bless it sounds like faith, but it would remain in the widow's sphere of control and creativity. Scripture makes the definition of faith clear in Hebrews 11:6. True faith is removed from human works and proposals. It is complete trust in and reliance on God.

Bringing our suggestions to God and asking Him to bless our creativity can be likened to Abraham asking God to bless his solution to God's promise (Genesis 17:18). God promised Abraham and Sarah a son, but in their desperation, they "created" their own answer to the problem of Sarah's barrenness – and after that presented their solution to God for His blessing. The difference in the sequence of events might be subtle, but for Abraham and the yet-to-be created nation of Israel, the outcome was different. God's plan for Israel was to be established through His miraculous opening of Sarah's womb, not via Hagar's womb.

Had the widow's jar of oil been presented to the Elisha before expressing her trust in God, she would have been asking God to bless her solution and not provide His answer to her problem. If we, reading this account thousands of years later as we are, were to follow her solution example, we will be opting for a natural answer to a spiritual problem. We need to be wary of following the same trajectory as Adam and Eve did and, relying on ourselves, set a disastrous course of independence from God.

Faith serves to glorify God and not our human wisdom or abilities. Faith starts where our human abilities, wisdom and experience end; where we place our total trust in God and wait for Him to answer. After petitioning God and waiting, His answer will come in a practical way. The important fact is that He will initiate His answer, not ours. When we initiate the answer, we will glorify it and ourselves.

If the widow had presented her jar of oil to the prophet to be blessed, it might have resulted in the jar of oil and the widow's smart thinking being elevated to the status if idols, or in the widow using the oil for nefarious purposes – after all, the nature of humanity is to attach emotional weight to perishable items. Similarly, Samson didn't frame or brand the donkey jawbone he used to kill Philistines with. He immediately discarded the weapon (Judges 15:17).

Elisha responded to the widow's needs as he did when he was handed the office of Elijah the prophet in 2 Kings 2:1-11. Elisha knew the anointing was from God, not from a man. His trust was anchored in God first and then in Elijah's cloak which he picked up and used to part the waters of the Jordan River. His appeal was to the Spirit of God to receive the double anointing. He understood that no person can accomplish the work of God unless God's Spirit anoints and appoints them.

Going back to the widow's request and the way she asked God for help, we can see an important principle for tackling our struggles. She first went to God with her problem through Elisha the man of God who represented her. Today we don't have to wait for a mediator to connect with God because Jesus is our mediator.

The human ego

It's sad to see how many well-known pastors have reframed the faith of believers to enrich themselves with worldly possessions, as can be seen in the lives of super-rich televangelists. It seems as if they've found a way to "print" money. They're like someone who has struck oil and will keep pumping the well to extract every drop they can. These televangelists' lifestyles and net worth speak for themselves – they may be rich in worldly wealth, but they're poor in the spirit.

If faith is meant to help the believer become more like the object of our faith, Jesus, then either the Bible or the televangelists are getting it wrong. Jesus spoke against worldly wealth; against riches that fade, rust and get stolen (Matthew 6:19-21). Jesus did not exemplify a king who set out to amass great worldly wealth for Himself.

We sometimes see pastors who, when faith projects bear fruit, congratulate themselves and forget that faith is a gift from God. The problem is that they set a poor example for their followers. What they say and do is emulated by their followers and instead of ensuring that Jesus is the object of every believer's faith, they become elevated and admired themselves and take the glory that is due to God (Isaiah 42:8).

Whenever the flesh is glorified, idolatry begins. When a person surrenders and calls on God to take over, His glory is revealed and He solves all man's problems. This is why faith brings glory to God and not man. The so-called faith pastors become self-absorbed and fall into Lucifer's trap, desiring glory for themselves. They create a theology where wealth and not the Gospel of Jesus Christ is the centre. What they forget is that in the life after this life every person will receive from God their rewards and judgements for things done in the flesh on earth (2 Corinthians 5:10).

When egos lead, people use their faith achievements as marketing stunts and before long, nothing is impossible anymore. These believers cross a dangerous line when they begin to command the Spirit of God.

Faith is initiated when people surrender and God is allowed to take control. If this were not so, then Ephesians 2:8,9 would not be true because salvation is one hundred percent the work of God and nothing can be attributed to the flesh. Therefore, when people do something in their own strength, it's not by faith and it does not please God. This includes the greatest feats of human ingenuity and creativity, which in many cases, are the result of humanity's hard work and not supernatural in nature at all.

Flesh or Spirit

Many years ago my son was building a sandcastle on the beach. After spending a lot of time constructing his work of art, he realised it would all be washed away when the tide came in. No matter how big the walls he built around his castle, the waves started pounding his castle and within a few minutes, all he had built was flattened. His efforts to protect his creation were doomed from the start. Such is a person who wages war using natural means to defend themself against an enemy who exists in the spirit. Minute after minute the small waves pounded the sandcastle. There were no large waves, but eventually my son gave up trying to rebuild his sand wall to protect his castle.

This story paints a picture of the believer who tries to walk his spiritual journey in his own strength and wisdom. The enemy's relentless attacks on people are like the constant motion of the waves that never cease. The devil never gives up trying to disrupt and derail the believer's spiritual growth. No matter how people may try, their enemy is a spiritual force and no flesh can stand against him. People are as weak and vulnerable against the enemy's persistent attacks as my son's sandcastle was against the persistent waves.

When the Apostle Paul says the righteous shall walk by faith, he's explaining that walking will include fighting (Romans 1:17). Nowhere in Scripture does it say that once a person gets saved, they can sit back and relax. In fact, we're warned that the attacks on a believer will gradually increase – see what happened to Job. No believer is exempt from the enemy's all-out hatred and jealousy. He is hell-bent on waging war against God's elect. He has focused his armies on every believer to kill, steal and destroy them (John 10:10). Jesus warned us to always be on our guard and never to be ignorant about the enemy's plans and schemes (Mark 13:33).

In Ephesians 6:16 Paul says we're to take up the shield of faith. Why a shield and why faith? A shield is for protection from the enemy's incoming arrows of doubt and unbelief. Interestingly, unbelief is like saying to God that we will fight the enemy in our own strength, the flesh. It's a clear and arrogant statement that we do not trust God's Word that instructs us about spiritual warfare (Ephesians 6:12). While the enemy is enticing us to fight him on his home turf using our own strength, faith is needed because the righteous shall walk by trusting God. This is another way of saying the righteous shall walk or live by faith.

Whenever the believer tries to "go it alone", their efforts always end in disaster. Jesus Himself warned us that we can do nothing without Him (John 15:5). When the believer tries to resist the enemy, they can only do so in the spirit, not on the flesh. Satan is a spirit and the flesh has no power over or against him. The natural person is totally blind to the things of the spirit world. Without being born again, the unsaved person remains blind. When they are born again, they begin to walk in the spirit, but need the guidance of God's Spirit to stay on the right path.

Faith, also expressed as trust in God, is needed so that the believer can navigate the world of the spirit. Here the Word of God is their light to put one foot in front of the other. The Word of God is always true, and if we obey His Word, we're expressing a trust in God. By doing so, God blesses the believer (Hebrews 11:6). The difference between going it alone in the flesh, and trusting God is that going it alone uses natural means to address a spiritual problem. When we walk by what God's Word says we rely on God to guide us. This is walking in the spirit – and when we do so, we're able to defeat the enemy who is a spirit.

The shield of faith means we surrender our problems to God and we hide in Him by following what His Word prescribes. It's important to remember that Jesus is both the Word of God (John 1:14) and the source and goal of our faith (Hebrews 12:2). The more of God's Word content we understand and know, the more accurately we will be able to follow God's commands.

In the Old Testament, God tabernacled among His people and they beheld His glory. Both Moses and Solomon experienced the presence of God and they constructed a place for God to be among His people. Obeying God was to maintain His presence with the people (Exodus 33:15) and the inverse was also true. In the New Testament God tabernacled among His people in the person of Jesus Christ who was God's glory manifested among His people. To obey God was to do everything Jesus commanded.

A good example of true faith is when Peter instantly obeyed Jesus' command to, 'Launch into the deep and let down your nets' (Luke 5:4). In doing so, Peter achieved a supernatural catch.

The flesh is helpless to solve our problems, while the spirit allows us to walk in the spirit world to supply all we need. Peter toiled the whole night in his own strength and caught nothing, but then he acted in the spirit and obeyed Jesus and caught an extraordinary amount.

Another excellent example of true faith took place at the wedding in Cana when Jesus turned water into wine (John 2:1-11). A key phrase here is when Mary told the servants: 'Do whatever He tells you' (John 2:5). An interesting statement is made in verse 11. It says Jesus revealed His glory and his disciples believed in Him. Obedience was the key to faith in God. Like the wedding servants, trusting God's Word and surrendering your science, arguments, worldly wisdom, expectations and all your efforts to Him will allow His glory to step in and solve their problem.

We might not have the same problem of our wine running out, which was a major concern for a seven-day Jewish wedding celebration. But our problems are equally impossible for us to address in the natural. We need supernatural interventions, and these only come when we call on God and are willing to lay our problems at His feet. At the same time, we must also be willing to obey what He commands us to do. This is where the flesh needs to be silenced, because the flesh will always argue and debate God's commands. In other words, we need to allow God to take control of our situation; we need to step out of the natural and step into the spiritual realm.

Both the examples of the wedding in Cana and Peter's large catch have three key steps. First, they exhausted their options and surrendered their human efforts to Jesus. Second, they abandoned their science and human wisdom. Third, they presented their problems to Jesus and obeyed His command. We can clearly see how the flesh has no place to accomplish anything in the presence of God.

Sorry I can't hear you

As mentioned above, one of the most powerful statements in the New Testament is when Jesus' mother Mary told servants at the wedding feast in Cana: 'Do whatever He tells you' (John 2:5).

Imagine the servants trying to come up with creative ideas to make more wine. Can you picture their dilemma? Are we not guilty of creatively coming up with our own ideas to provide more wine? Mary's statement is a key aspect to understanding faith. In the five words she spoke, she revealed all we need to grow in our trust in God and why some believers' faith does not work. Mary told the servants to act on the words of Jesus – nothing more nor less.

Acting on Jesus' words meant the servants had to resign their ideas, their past experiences, cultural wisdom, their scientific calculations and all their prejudices. They had to regard the unknown Jesus higher than the master of the wedding banquet.

Putting this event into today's terms, we need to act on what Jesus said. It's not so straightforward because He's not present with us in the flesh. However, we have His Word and His Spirit leading and guiding us. Isn't it true what He said to His disciples in John 14? Through His Spirit He will always be with us (John 14:16).

Chapter 15

How faith develops in the believer

As a pastor I'm often asked for help by church members. These requests vary from financial assistance and help with starting a business to discussing who single people should date or marry, marital problems, tension between parents and their children and many more. Jesus Himself said that we will always have people around us who need help (Matthew 26:11), but that solving people's daily needs was not the focus of His incarnation. Jesus' main incarnation goal was to take away the sins of the world (Matthew 1:21). His focus was on bringing redemption to the world to meet humanity's greatest need.

People primarily have two types of needs – earthly and spiritual. Their most basic earthly needs are food, water, air and shelter. What salvation provides is the fulfilment of the most basic spiritual need. When our earthly needs are met, it doesn't mean our spiritual needs are also met. But when our spiritual needs are met, it could mean that our earthly needs get met a lot easier. Any believer, post-salvation, will still have daily earthly needs, but they have walked through the door of salvation and now they're living in a new spiritual realm (Proverbs 3:5,6). This new realm doesn't cancel out the daily realities experienced by the believer. But it empowers the believer to approach God for their daily earthly needs, something they were never able to do previously. Before salvation, the individual had to provide for themselves through their own strength, their own limited knowledge and acquired natural resources. Once saved, the realm of the spirit is accessible to the believer to receive everything they need (Matthew 6:28-34).

The requests I often get are from new converts who have received the blessing of salvation, but they lack the development phase in their faith. They're unable to trust God for their daily needs and for answers to their challenges. Salvation faith, mentioned in Ephesians 2:8,9, does not require much from a believer. The conviction of sin, brought by the Spirit of God, is a strong power and most of the work to achieve salvation is done by God Himself.

Compared with receiving salvation by faith, walking by faith to receive daily needs can be a real challenge for the believer. This is true because up to the point of salvation, the individual has always relied on themselves to supply their own needs. It's easier to call the pastor to ask for help than praying and waiting on God to supply their needs. This is the most difficult phase for any new believer in their faith walk, but it's a vital part of the believer's development. Scripture provides us with an excellent example when Israel left Egyptian slavery and began their journey through the Wilderness. The exodus from Egypt was a demonstration of God's power and then, after their liberation, the Wilderness began a new phase for the people of God when they had to learn how to depend on God's provision and protection. We can see Israel's cry for human support as they argue with Moses, their pastoral figure, to return to the easy way of living they enjoyed back in Egypt. Everything was supplied to them, yet they were in slavery. It was an easy existence when it came to their daily needs (Numbers 11:5).

As in Israel's case, breaking a person's self-reliance requires a season of hunger to force them to depend on God. Becoming reliant on God and not on self is a process the human mind fails to understand or agree with. Self-reliance was the initial lie Satan sold Adam and Eve. He managed to convince them to walk away from God and become their own source of supply (Genesis 3:5). People were not created by God to be self-reliant, because, as discussed earlier, people have both natural and spiritual needs and they're unable to fulfil their spiritual needs from the natural realm. Only God can satisfy spiritual needs. It's for this reason that God called every believer to walk by faith – also understood as trusting God. Once the believer has stepped out of the natural realm of self-reliance, a new world of trusting God opens. It's the supernatural world, the world of the spirit, where God's supplies water from a rock in a desert; bread every morning – and all His people are required to do is trust Him.

A single focus

Too many cooks spoil the broth and too many advisers confuse the decision-maker. These examples explain the principle that singular focus is more likely to ensure a successful outcome than multiple focuses. Hebrews 12:2 says we are to fix our eyes on Jesus, the author and perfector of our faith.

Since the beginning of time, people have developed and explored many avenues to fill the deep desire within themselves to reach out to a higher power. This desire originates from God and can only be filled by Him and humanity has been given the Word of God to tell them who God is and what He expects from them.

However, humanity is also bombarded with options for knowledge and inspiration – Buddhism, Islam, humanism, scientology, ancestral worship and many other cults throughout history – but all these options are mere mirages on the road to eternal death. There's no other way in which people can undo their eternal dilemma of sin (Matthew 1:21; John 3:3; 1 Corinthians 2:4). Jesus is our only hope and the only way to be reborn and to grow to maturity.

Eyes fixed on Jesus

How does a person keep their eyes fixed on Jesus in a world full of deceptive and false solutions to their problems? The Father has given us Jesus who is His Word (John 1:1,2). The Spirit of Jesus not only implants the Word in our hearts like seeds, but He also empowers the Word to grow within us (Colossians 2:7). The more of the Word we have within us, the more we will be inclined to yield to the Spirit's will.

It's not that there are no other options to solve humanity's problems and supply their needs; there are many, but what Hebrews says in 12:2 is that we need to fix our eyes on a single focus – Jesus. By reading, studying and understanding the Word of God, who is Jesus Christ made available to us by the Spirit of God, we begin to focus our attention on the Word to direct our steps. Our decision-making capabilities will be directed by the Spirit to understand what pleases God and to remain standing in testing times. Despite the difficult times He faced, Jesus focused on the task ahead of Him, knowing what the Father had tasked Him to do. He was not distracted by fine-sounding arguments, worldly promises nor by the frustrations He suffered; there's no better person for us to emulate and build our hopes on.

Despite the worldviews that existed in Jesus' time, He focused on His Father's plan to remove sin from His people. No other goal was more important because it was the only goal that His Father was interested in. It was God's highest goal to set His people free from sin slavery so that they can worship Him in spirit and in truth.

God was not interested in increasing people's IQ or their wealth, nor was He interested in political world peace. He was focused on one goal – ending the eternal effects of sin, not eradicating it from the earth. Sin has been with us since Adam's fall, but its effect on the believer is being reversed. Having a single focus and making that the goal of Jesus' incarnation on earth, ensured that Jesus achieved the Father's goal and that it's a singular goal that people are able to pursue.

Fixing their eyes on Jesus, the Word of God, requires that a person says no to other ideas, philosophies, human ideologies and worldviews. No one else can remove sin but God, and no one can mature a person towards holiness but God. The salvation plan of God targets sin and it is the door to achieving holiness. No person can purify themselves in any other way but by believing in Jesus Christ. Today, as in history, people have many clever ideas to make them better than they are. These ideas originate with fallen humanity and they use a multifaceted approach to improve people and their fortunes. It's incorrect to claim that we are pressured to respond to the distractions we face. As living by faith is a volitional walk, so is the decision to say no to the world's offers to become a better person. Sin has polluted people and the entire creation and the undoing of sin is the only answer to humanity's dilemma as to the restoration of all creation.

Eternity with God is only possible if sin is undone in that person's life. When someone is reborn, they're made new by the power of God through the message of salvation. God set out to reconcile people back to Himself after they fell away in sin and they need to understand that and align themselves to God's purpose.

Faith, as a gift from the Spirit of God, is working in the heart of the believer to achieve what the person in their own strength and wisdom cannot accomplish. Faith, as explained earlier, is not given to us to achieve what is naturally possible for us to achieve; it's given to us to achieve spiritual results – something we are unable to achieve. If faith is used to pursue worldly wealth outside of God's will, which people have done, that's a blatant abuse of this amazing gift.

God's plan of salvation is achieved by the nature and power of His Word, represented and enacted by Jesus, and affected in us by His Holy Spirit.

When we suffer a setback, we tend recognise the same scenario when it arises again and we take precautions to prevent it happening again. I want to suggest the inverse principle applies to faith.

When an unbeliever hears the Word of God and feels the call of God on their lives, they act on the call, using the gift of faith that the Spirit of God placed in their hearts. Faith allows them to reach out to God during the salvation message to receive justification. The same spiritual gift of faith, after being deposited in the person's heart, now begins to develop like a seed sprouting and breaking though the surface to reach the sunlight. Initially the little faith plant is weak and might struggle with obstacles and challenges around it, but it will grow with time. What it needs is a single breakthrough to develop a sense of strength and become resolute. It takes one victory in the face of great opposition and the believer's faith becomes their compass. Where they drifted in the past, this one seminal event in their faith walk will transform their faith into an indestructible force. They will turn into resilient believers who do not walk by what they see or hear, but by the guidance of the Spirit of faith.

Unfortunately, for some believers this force becomes a distraction and can lead to their destruction. A powerful faith capability can become an idol within a person's spiritual journey, where they begin to apply it to serve carnal desires and not spiritual pursuits. It is therefore crucial to maintain a healthy balance between the gift of faith, other spiritual gifts and the fruit of the Spirit.

Navel gazing

Not long ago I attended a meeting where the theme of the presentation was about decision-making in difficult times. Halfway through the presentation, an image was projected on the screen of earth from a vantage point deep in space. The earth looked tiny and insignificant and I could barely make out the continents. The presenter stated that our problems are as insignificant and that we make more of them than we should. This told me that my problems are insignificant. Well, I was upset. No matter how far the speaker zoomed out to make my situation look small and insignificant, my problems were real. The financial hardship I was experiencing had significant generational risks attached to it. There was absolutely nothing I could do to free myself from the stranglehold I was experiencing. No matter which direction I turned to, it made no difference. The predicament I found myself in was not even my own making. Make no mistake: my problems were not insignificant – they were real; very real. The mere notion that I would feel better when shown how insignificant I am and how meaningless my problems were made me feel even more desperate.

I sat with my head dropped down, gazing at my navel – not because I had nothing to look at, but because I felt desperate and alone in my struggle. I needed a miracle and I needed it urgently. Telling me that my problems were insignificant did not help me. I felt numb and my tired brain did not feel able to come up with a solution.

A few weeks later I was in church and the preacher stated that we all face difficult times, and then I was pleasantly surprised by his main idea; he said he didn't want to teach people how faith works because, as a mature audience, we've all heard teachings on faith. But what he said next hit me so hard that I felt that I needed to ask God for forgiveness in my struggles. He read 2 Samuel 5:19, where David approaches God for advice and strength.

> … so David inquired of the Lord, 'Shall I go and attack the Philistines? Will you deliver them into my hands?' The Lord answered him, 'Go, for I will surely deliver the Philistines into your hands.' (NIV)

What transpires is that David finds strength in God and at the same time he's assured of a victory. David fixed his eyes, not on his navel area as I had, but on God. By elevating God, David's problems were not insignificant; they were real and had deadly consequences should he lose the battle. His problems were immense, but by looking to God he established his faith in something greater than his problem. He made God the centre of his focus for help to overcome the enemy.

David didn't learn a new skill, gather more men, grew in his battle experience, nor did he change his battle tactics. No, he didn't add anything. He made God the authority over the battle and in doing so, his enemy became insignificant. Nothing can compare to God or His armies. David put his request before God and humbled himself under God's command. David did not sit down in pity to navel gaze. He lifted his eyes to see the God of glory, the everlasting all present deliverer of Israel. He placed his trust in the One who cannot lie. He had the assurance of a victory with God fighting for him.

When we encounter difficulties for which we have no answer, resources or strength to handle, know that God is busy opening up new areas of authority to you. He wants to develop your walk in the spirit. Unfortunately, many believers see challenges as demonic or because of past mistakes and they don't learn anything from them. Don't sit and navel gaze. Lift up your eyes and acknowledge the greatness of God. This will turn your struggle into joy, and although your problems are big, there is someone bigger than your problems to take care of them.

Chapter 16

Growing in faith

G rowing up in the seventies and eighties, I couldn't help but hear the constant droning on radio and later television about the faith movement coming out of the USA. Evangelists punted the idea of faith being a force you exercise like a muscle to obtain anything you desire. It was a message that, in my personal view, led many people astray – not necessarily into the occult, but into avenues of selfish ambition and fleshly fulfilment. These preachers even related conversations about how God spoke to them in person to not be content with what they have and to keep pushing for bigger and better material things. On the outside, the material wealth of these preachers seemed to back up their claims.

Is the faith they professed and the way they applied it what God says in His Word? Is that what we should be striving for as Christians who are looking towards our reward in heaven? Or are we being led astray today by the same teachings that urge people to proclaim, decree and declare things God has not purposed for them to say, own and do? Has faith been misapplied?

When looking at the principle of faith, Scripture reveals that faith is not a self-fulfilment project. Faith does not work like a muscle you exercise to get it to grow larger, as some of the faith movement pastors explained. In fact, Scripture says that faith is a process whereby the believer becomes less and Jesus becomes more. The true test of faith is: can you remove the object of your faith, what you're hoping for, and place Jesus there? If you can, then your faith is pure. However, if you cannot place Jesus in the centre of your faith aim, your faith is misguided and your aim is selfish gain.

Why do I say faith can be misguided? Well, people often use single verses in Scripture and not a whole Bible understanding to explain faith. This has led many believers astray. Principles like faith do not function in a vacuum. When we stand on a single isolated verse, we're not reading it in its proper context. It's equally important to know that the main purpose of Scripture is to glorify God and not the fulfilment of man's fleshly desires. Furthermore, if the believer does not know that the narrative throughout Scripture is reconciliation between God and man, they will build their house on sand. They will misuse faith and end up glorifying people. In failing to apply the basic Bible interpretation principles, believers are led astray into pursuing earthly goals and not heavenly treasures.

From Genesis to Revelation, faith is part of God's plan of reconciliation. God is busy establishing a relationship with every believer, using faith as the key ingredient. When Jesus explained this to Nicodemus in John 3:16, He wanted the teacher of Israel to see how God came to establish a link between heaven and earth. God gave His Son as a reconciliatory sacrifice and the spiritual gift of faith allows every person to be reconciled to God. Believing in Jesus is what saves us and invites us into the relationship God desires with each believer. This very gift of faith begins to work in us to systematically purify us and create a growing divide between us and the world. If faith is misrepresented, it systematically causes people to drift away from God – even though their works might seem amazing. Faith is meant to be a reconciliatory tool, not a force the flesh uses to obtain wealth. Scripture says God made Abraham rich (Genesis 14:23), which was the blessing of God; a reward for his faith. It was not his faith that enabled him to get rich.

Total reliance

Faith can be expressed as total reliance on someone to do what we cannot do for ourselves. It operates at its best when we surrender our lives to someone who has covenanted to save us. Faith accomplishes the impossible task of saving a lost person (Ephesians 2:8-9). To save a person, salvation faith is needed because it's impossible for a lost person to save themselves.

This is not where faith ends and the person must then begin to walk by faith (Romans 1:17) to undergo the transformation into Christlikeness. Faith is given to establish an eternal attribute of being faithful to God's commands within a believer. Living by faith can also be described as living faithfully or being trustworthy (1 Corinthians 4:2). Every believer, at every stage of their lives, at any given stage or time, is going through a process of change. Through the washing by God's Word and the leading of the Spirit of God, the believer begins to resemble the nature and character of Jesus. This a result of the progressive removal of sin and its effects in the believer.

Romans 1:5 speaks of the "obedience that comes from faith". The outworking of faith is the desire it creates in the heart of the believer to obey God's Word. Sin is the greatest enemy of a believer's relationship with God and faith is there to keep the believer from sin. The requirement of faith is that the believer walks pure before God, which we in Genesis 15:6 when God proclaimed Abraham righteous. In Genesis 17:1. God expected obedience from Abraham, which can be seen in Scripture when God asked him to sacrifice his son.

Jesus used faith and trust interchangeably in John 14:1. When speaking about a relationship, it's easier to understand the principles of trust between two people. It also makes us appreciate the effects of sin in a relationship and the broken trust that is the result. In this instance, what God expected from Abraham was to walk without sin, meaning, do not violate the relationship. Obedience to God's will and Word keeps us free from sin and it allows us to prosper in our relationship with Him.

A relationship between two people can only exist when it is based on trust. So when a non-human object is introduced and becomes the focus of one of the party, the relationship will suffer. Faith was never meant to increase personal wealth or anchor people deeper into this broken world and what it offers. If that were true, faith would be counterproductive to our relationship with God. Faith can accomplish great feats in the life of a believer, but its focus is to initiate and strengthen the believer's relationship with God – not with this broken world.

Jesus Himself equated friendship with the world as war with God (James 4:4). Jesus also instructed His disciples not to take much with them on their journey (Luke 22:35), and Paul said worldly possessions will be a snare (1 Timothy 6:9). Faith seeks to empty the believer of any self-reliance, worldly lust and boasting. The emptier the believer, the more the person can be filled by the Spirit of God. When this happens, the person can acquire great wealth, as Abraham did, and yet walk humbly with God. Faith is not a tool given to us to enhance the gathering of possessions in this world, nor has it been given to us to impoverish us. Should God decide to bless the believer with great wealth, it's God's blessing and not faith that accomplished it.

The essence of Hebrews 4:2 is that Jesus gives birth to faith in our hearts to believe in Him, which is echoed in Romans 10:17. Jesus as the Word begins to dwell in us as we walk, stumble and run in our spiritual development. Eventually, as eternity with God takes place either by death or the rapture, faith has done its work and is no longer needed. 1 Corinthians 13:9-13 says that the imperfect will be replaced by the perfect. It says that of hope, faith and love, only love will remain, which explains that the purpose of faith is to lead us to an eternal relationship with God. Perfection comes when we are with God and faith is no longer needed to accomplish this. Faith has done its work and is now obsolete.

Wrong teaching

Where teachers of the faith movement get it wrong is to focus their followers on what faith can achieve for them on this earth. By using several isolated Scripture verses, they distort the application of faith. Faith can, when mixed with human talents and ambition, achieve incredible feats. However, we're not called to achieve in the material realm, but in the spiritual realm. Material possessions, at best, are distractions. If you were to do a sanity check on believers who have totally embraced the faith movement's principles, you will see the ideology that God is a "mother" whose sole purpose is to supply when and what they subjectively need. These misleading principles have been followed by many believers as a result of loud and ambitious pastors and presumptuous churches who totally lack personal Bible study. They lazily take whatever is in front of them. The faith movement, like many other movements in history, takes one aspect of Scripture and makes it the focus. They aim to solve a societal expectation and in doing so, they move away from the purpose of faith.

The faith movement originated at a time when the US economy was struggling and believers were bombarded by televangelists who promised them an end to their problems. The message was that they had to sow money to reap money. Money was the televangelist's tool of the trade. It became the focus of the faith movement's preachers and their followers, and material wealth skyrocketed among these believers. They approached God to get from Him what they needed – desperate believers will swallow any teaching without first verifying its origin and accuracy.

These believers have an overdeveloped reliance on only a few Bible verses, but lack an overall understanding of the purpose of their salvation. In this instance, selfish ambition has replaced the Great Commission.

Author and perfector of our faith

Hebrews 12:2 says Jesus is the author and perfector of our faith. This doesn't refer to principles of increasing our wealth and attaining our fleshly desires. The goal of our faith is a secure, solid and mature relationship with God. To explain this we can use the metaphor of a recently married couple. If their single aim is to work hard to accumulate as much wealth as possible, the result will be the end of their relationship and they would have totally missed the purpose of the marriage. They've grown, but in the wrong area, and the result will be the loss of the most precious thing of all.

Similarly, the faith movement's principles cling to worldly possessions and a continuous desire for more. Those who delve into these misleading branches of Christianity have their love for God replaced by a love for the things of this world and their only growth is in accumulating bigger and better dust-collectors.

Growing in faith doesn't refer to the material things we can accumulate in this world, or to say it another way, faith is not about growing horizontally, but rather vertically. Horizontal growth refers to gathering what this world offers. Vertical growth refers to our relationship with God. The principal of horizontal versus vertical growth is clearly depicted by what is said in Hebrews 12. The ancient believers were commended, not for their worldly possessions, but for the lack thereof. He encourages every believer to emulate the heroes of faith who remained steadfast despite severe trials. Interestingly, none of the heroes of the faith received worldly possessions as their reward. They received a heavenly kingdom – a reward that can never be taken away.

Jesus said our Father in heaven will supply our needs (Matthew 6:25-34 NIV). In verse 33, Jesus said, "seek first God's kingdom and His righteousness" before we focus on what we need. He is saying that within the safety of our post-salvation relationship with God, our needs will be met, suggesting that the relationship the believer has with God takes precedence over any needs we might have. Jesus assured us that God is faithful and will not let us down. It's also noteworthy that Jesus spoke of what we need and not what we want.

The relationship of trust we're offered by God is so important to Him that He sealed His promise by an oath in His Son's blood (Luke 22:20). Trust is a big issue to God. In Deuteronomy 1:32, Israel's distrust is highlighted as one of the main reasons why that generation was not allowed to enter the Promised Land. In Hebrews 4:2, the author mentions the account of Israel's distrust again. The Israelites didn't benefit from God's complete plan of salvation because they had no faith in Him.

Faith in God is a personal choice made by a believer, and distrust in God is a very personal insult. In John 14:1 Jesus assures the disciples that God will take care of them despite a bleak future facing His imminent departure. Jesus' words were remarkable; He wanted to reaffirm their trust in God. Then He told them to also trust Him. Jesus is God, and He's worthy of our complete trust.

When we understand that faith and trust go together, the importance of the relationship we have with God becomes even clearer. Within this relationship, trust is the foundation and obedience is the fruit of our trust. Trust gets us into the relationship with God and obedience keeps us in it. Historically, when Israel fell into disobedience, their next step was distrust in God, which was followed by God's discipline and withdrawal from the relationship (see Exodus 32:9-10 and Exodus 33:2-3). A clear example is the account in Genesis 3:1-5 where Adam abandoned his trust in God and instead placed his trust in the serpent.

Chapter 17

Seasons in our faith journey

F aith deals exclusively with things beyond human ability. The gift of God (1 Corinthians 12:9 and Ephesians 2:8-9) is the great enabler, which allows us to achieve what God calls us to and in ways He allows us to. There is an important difference between faith and obedience. In Luke 17:7-10, Jesus instructed His disciples about when to believe and when to act in obedience. One of the sequential steps of living by faith is acting out what we believe. We see this when Jesus called the lame man to rise, pick up his bed and walk (John 5:8-16). When healing the lepers, Jesus instructed them to go and show themselves to the priests. Scripture says as they turned and walked away, they were healed (Luke 17:14). The sick man who was lowered through the roof of a house was healed because of the faith of his friends (Luke 5:17-20).

Faith is the door created by God for us so that we can walk through it into a new, supernatural life on earth. It ushers us from a natural thinking existence to a spiritually ruled existence. We must fight to remain hopeful. If you begin to distrust God because of delays, frustration will set in and you will begin to argue with God.

The fulfilment of our request forms a solid foundation for us to stand on and it becomes irrefutable proof to us and to others. Such proof is our guarantee of God's faithfulness, His reliability and believability. Not only does Scripture reveal God's proven track record to Israel in the Old Testament, the church in the New Testament, but to us in person.

The blessing of faith

Here's a clear illustration about entering God's rest. Imagine a man in a tiny boat on a rough seas being tossed about by the enormous waves that dwarf his small boat. He is terrified and thinks he has no hope and no way of surviving the storm. Suddenly a large ship appears next to him and because of its size, the waves have no effect on it. The waves that dwarfed the boat are dwarfed by the ship. Everyone on the ship is safe and secure and no one is tossed about by the storm. The captain is experienced had he has faced many storms; he's not threatened by the size of the waves because he knows his vessel can withstand them. The ship comes alongside the man's small boat and the captain calls out to him to come on board – there's room for him. If he accepts the captain's invitation, his anxiety and fear will end in an instant – he will be safe and he will be at peace. Why would the man in the boat refuse the captain's invitation? Wouldn't it be foolish of the man to choose to remain in his small boat to face the storm on his own? On the ship, the man could engage in activities that could lead to his development and progress because the captain would be facing every storm on behalf of all those on his big ship.

The difference between fighting for survival and living a peaceful life of progress is one decision. Give up your own efforts and climb onboard the captain's large vessel. He knows more than you and the sheer size of his ship means he can weather any storm.

The blessings of a walk of faith

Faith releases a blessing to every believer who chooses to depend on God. To be blessed means to be empowered beyond what people can do for themselves. A blessing is like water in the desert, like food during a famine, like healing received after a terminal prognosis from a doctor. A blessing is received as a reward for choosing to walk by faith.

Hebrews 11:6 says that God rewards those who put their trust or faith in Him without seeing His face. It is a gift from God; a gift that has no origin in this world and is God's favour in the face of impossibilities.

The more a person walks by faith, the more they experience the promise of God, which begins with the foundation of salvation, "By grace through faith." Grace means an undeserved gift when we place our trust in God. When we receive God's gift, we stop trying to prove that we did something to deserve it.

The effect of faith is that we enter God's rest (Hebrews 4:1-11) and we hand over the Lordship of our lives to Jesus. By doing this, we enter God's rest on earth daily. Living in this rest, we are not pressured to do things to prove our worth anymore.

Without faith we are a people beset by anxiety and fear, and to escape it, we embark on earthly project to feel valued and deserving of a reward. The more we engage in these manmade activities, the more we shut God out.

The rest of God is reflected in the Genesis account of creation. God worked for six days and on the seventh day He rested. The fourth commandment is about resting, trusting God and allowing Him to be the ruler in our lives.

> Remember the Sabbath day by keeping it holy. Exodus 20:8 (NIV)

To continue working hard for what we need is the opposite of what God promised when He invited us into His rest.

Whether using gifting or talents

Faith, as we have learnt, is a surrender to everything people can achieve in their own strength, talents and wisdom, but it doesn't take away a person's responsibility to do the normal tasks they have to do daily. Faith is to achieve the impossible. When people employ their human talents, personal success binds them to one sphere of human potential, while faith elevates them to God's sphere of achievement. What stands between human achievement and Godly potential is a person's willingness to lay down their personal success.

There are many things that people can accomplish that might not be what God expects them to do. Their success through their human efforts could be their greatest hindrance in doing what God had planned. In all cases, faith is the power to achieve what is impossible to us as humans.

Even if we accomplish something incredible through human effort, it could still be something God did not ordain for us to achieve. Hebrews 11:6 makes it clear that to please God, everything we do must be done in faith. As explained earlier, faith can be used interchangeably with trust. If we're going to do something by trusting God, it means we need Him to do it for us, otherwise we could have done it ourselves.

Aaron's Golden Calf

What is the significance of the golden calf that Moses' brother, Aaron, made for the people of Israel? Does it contain a warning for us living in today's modern world? To understand Israel's reason for asking for an idol to worship, we must go back and look at Israel's years under Egyptian slavery. Overnight, the life they had always known was no more. The rituals they had borrowed from the Egyptians, the idol worship, the sacrifices and traditions they had inherited were left behind in Egypt, but they carried these Egyptian-pagan beliefs with them in their hearts and minds. Their sense of security was anchored in these idols and what they hoped to get from them in time of need.

The Egyptians's idol worship was founded on the source of their food and livelihood – the Nile River and its seasonal flooding, which kept the banks fertile. The people of Egypt were dependent on their agriculture and believed they had to appease the gods to bless their crops and livestock. Sacrifices, idol worship and many other practices filled the Egyptians' daily lives.

The need for food security meant the Egyptians crafted many gods to worship in the hope that they would bless the worshippers. This meant that the Jewish people in Egypt followed many of these practices, honouring the gods who "provided" the blessings of rain and good crops. It all boiled down to the crucial aspect of trust. The Israelites felt they needed a god who could lead and protect them and provide all they needed. They were worried about the future. And so they exchanged the trust that God offered them, the invitation to enter His rest, as Moses explained in Exodus 32:8, for a lifeless handmade idol. God wanted them to place their trust in Him. He wanted to provide for them, protect them, guide and lead them. Instead, they carved an image out of gold and worshipped it. It's not surprising God was very angry with them. He even went as far as saying to Moses He was going to kill them all and start over with Moses.

It seemed as if Moses, the man who had led them up to that point, had died on the mountain. Who was going to lead them now? Moses had taken them out Egypt and its food into the desert where there was no water. They became angry with Moses, accusing him of leading them out into the desert to die. Their Egyptian upbringing and context were threatened as God stepped in to be their leader, guide, lawgiver, protector and provider.

The golden calf was a symbol of Israel's time in Egypt. But this idol had nothing to do with Israel's history; it had everything to do with an attempt to secure the future. This was the very set of beliefs the Egyptians had – they hoped that when they died they would have secured a safe passage into the next life through their efforts on earth. For this reason, they were a polytheistic people and they made many sacrifices to the many gods they worshipped.

The story of Aaron's golden calf is a clear message to every Christian. Put your trust in God. He has the future in His hand. Believe in Him because in Him your future is secure.

God's biggest complaint against Israel as they journeyed from Egypt to the Promised Land, was their expressed distrust in Him (Numbers 14-15; Hebrews 4:2). Trust is a very personal and deep emotion, whether it is given or received. Refusing to trust someone even though they have shown that they can be trusted, is a slap in the person's face.

Chapter 18

Why not trust God?

The inverse of Paul's statement in Romans 1:17 – the righteous shall walk by faith – is that the unrighteous shall walk by sight, or said in another way, they shall trust in themselves or something else tangible.

Walking by faith is trusting in the Almighty God, the creator and sustainer of the universe. It means placing your total hope and life in His hands. This brings incredible rest and peace to the believer. The opposite is also true. Placing your trust and belief in yourself, in an idol, a set of laws or in another person, can only bring on incredible fear, anxiety and an uncertain future. Faith in anything else but God has been proven to fail.

Paul's statement also highlights what it's like for a person before they are declared righteous by grace through faith. Up to the point of their salvation, they've had no secure anchor in their lives. They might appear successful, perhaps they've gained great wealth through hard work or they might have a resume that shows great academic achievements. In many instances, people view those who head up big and successful organisations as having achieved the pinnacle of success. This is where the world makes a great mistake. Worldly achievements, no matter how big, mean nothing to God.

His Word spells out clearly what gets His attention. In Hebrews 11:6 we read that God rewards those who approach Him in faith. He's not interested in human achievement because He enables humans to achieve what they so ignorantly boast about.

Transformation process

To fully appreciate what it means to trust in something other than the living God, we need to understand human behaviour and the power of the mind. Salvation, as explained, is not a once-off event; it's a lifelong process. At the point of justification when the believer is made righteous before God is the start of the process.

God expects justification and the sanctification of the whole person, which includes the renewing of the person's soul and mind. Romans 12:2 says we're not to follow the world's way.

> Do not conform to the pattern of this world, but be trans-
> formed by the renewing of your mind. Then you will be
> able to test and approve what God's will is—his good,
> pleasing and perfect will. (NIV)

What then is the world's way? It's simply to rely on its systems and beliefs that people are their own destiny and saviour. In the same verse Paul says we must undergo a transformation of our carnal mindsets and beliefs. People cannot depend on themselves to secure their own future. This is what the world promotes. God expects the opposite from us. He sent His Son to die for us, to enable us to put to death the idea that people can be their own source of wisdom. Jesus died, was buried in the tomb and was raised on the third day so that we can put to death the carnal mind that has been our god. According to Romans 8:11, the Holy Spirit was the power that raised Jesus from the dead and that same Spirit enables us to overcome one of our greatest stumbling blocks, which is our carnal minds. Every time we need to decide to obey God, we will be faced with a challenge to follow our own minds.

If we look at the behaviour of the Israelites who escaped Egyptian slavery, the 400 years that they lived among the Egyptians and soaked up their religious practices, idol worship and lifestyle, had a deep impact on them and they could not remove themselves from the Egyptian influences and they were introduced to visible representatives of so-called deities. Worship did not coincide with faith, because what you saw was what you put your faith in.

Idols were visible and tangible and the worshipper could decide the length, the way and the nature of the worship. Worshipping an idol was gratifying because it allowed the worshipper to boast in their "holy" deeds. This worship was not spiritual at all; it was flesh elevating a being created by the flesh.

Despite the religious influences of the Egyptians in the lives of the Israelites, the hope of the fulfilment of the Abrahamic promise kept the nation going. The night of the Passover was the next step in the fulfilment of their dream of their own land, their own government, and their right to self-determination. Their identity as God's people was about to take shape.

Their dream of a land of their own was temporarily overshadowed by the realities of their history in Egypt and their view of the one true God was obscured by their desperate desire for a leader they could see and touch. They grew up with visible gods, manmade idols, that represented different facets of life.

It was therefore not surprising when Moses stayed on the mountain with God for forty nights and days, that the Israelites wanted a leader they could see. Their old habits surfaced. They provoked God, their Saviour and Father, to the point of wanting to wipe them out. God was ready to remove them and start over with Moses to build another nation.

Israel's temporary needs overshadowed God's promises to them. The harshness of the Wilderness made them reconsider their position as a free nation under God and they were unhappy with their circumstances (Exodus 14:11; Numbers 16:13). Whenever challenges arose, they remembered their days in slavery and wanted to return there, claiming that life was easy there. They forgot that they had no spiritual authority, no dominion (Genesis 1:26-28) in Egypt. They didn't have God leading them and walking among them. They could not determine their own destiny. But their desire in the Wilderness was for fleshly gratification, food, water and shelter. They didn't understand that God had liberated them from slavery, spiritual domination and oppression. He set them on a path to freedom, rest and fulfilment – everything contained in the Abrahamic promise in Genesis 12:1-3.

They wanted something they could see, touch and relate to. God speaking to them with a loud voice, from a dark mountain, scared them and they could not relate to Him. And what made things even more difficult, was that their ancestors spoke of a Promised Land, but the difficulties they faced prevented them from seeing a way out of slavery. Moses knew it was going to be difficult to convince them to believe his message that he was sent by God to liberate them from slavery. Visible gods made them feel secure – and God's message to them through Moses was that trusting Him in the inside would secure them externally. This was the message of believing in God and trusting in His provision, His protection and His leadership.

Faith requires all of me

There are many questions that are often asked by Christians. Why are we not walking with the same measure of supernatural demonstrations that the apostles did? Why do we not see the same effects if we pray for people who have medical conditions? Why do we not command things and immediately see answers? Have we perhaps lost our faith in God to deliver us and provide what we need? Are we depending on ourselves for what can only be achieved in the Spirit?

Faith in God enables us to be saved, to mature spiritually and enter our eternal dwelling place with God. By faith we wake up in the morning, by faith we walk during the day through all our challenges and by faith we lay our heads down at night to sleep. We are to live by faith in the One who knows what tomorrow holds.

To answer the question of the difference between the apostles' and our abilities, we must look at the definition of faith. We have established that faith and trust are interchangeable.

When Jesus came from heaven to earth, He had already surrendered His will and life even before He was born in a humble manger. To take Jesus' surrender a further step, He said He only acts when His Father instructs Him and only speaks the words His Father asks Him to speak.

In Genesis we read about the two trees in the Garden of Eden. From then, God started by instructing humanity in the choice of obedience. God will never force anyone to do anything. The very basis of faith is a choice we exercise. Faith is a surrendering of all we are, all we can do and all we want to do. Faith should lead to obedience, which requires a wilful surrender of our will. We see the clearest expression of faith when Jesus, fully God and fully man, departs from heaven to serve His Father's desire to save humanity from sin. The surrender Jesus demonstrated was a surrender of His all, even unto death. This total surrender allows His Father to work through Him. To the extent that we surrender, to that extent God can work through us.

Let me explain this principle of surrender using a practical example. A glass half full of dirty water can only accommodate a half measure of clean water. Once filled, the vessel will contain both clean and dirty water, but it will still be dirty water and not very useful. To achieve the desired clean water results, the glass must be emptied of its contents, washed, and then filled with clean water. This, I believe, is why the apostles were able to do powerful works. They were emptied of themselves and filled with the nature and character of Jesus. His Word dwelt in them richly and the Spirit did not have to rival fleshly pursuits to work in and through them. In the minds of the apostles, they were "dead already". They fully understood the road Jesus travelled; a road that led to death of the flesh and resurrection to eternal life. This is after all what baptism in water symbolises to Christian believers – death to the flesh and alive to Christ.

Once a person has tasted the power of God and equally, the futility and folly of people's wisdom and reasoning, they will increasingly rely on the Spirit for everything they do and need. Until we've emptied ourselves of our own fleshly desires, will and wisdom, the Spirit of God is not able to work through us as He desires. It is as if we get in His way. Paul says it like this:

> I have been crucified with Christ and I no longer live, but Christ lives in me. Galatians 2:20a (NIV)

Pressure aids development

I once read about a famed scientist who lived his life as an atheist. He didn't pronounce his unbelief in a higher power because, in his view, science was all humanity needed. His hope for a better world was that science would come up with all the answers and that only time was needed before science would deliver what humanity would need in perpetuity. This scientist became ill and no matter how he reasoned, science couldn't cure him. He wanted science to deliver what he needed, which was a cure for his disease. As one of the engineers who designed the Apollo moon-mission thruster rockets, he was proud of the moon-landing mission and all that it represented in exceptional research and development by engineers to escape the earth's gravitational pull and to travel to the moon. It had never been done and the old way of building rockets had had to change.

On his deathbed the famed scientist had a breakthrough and he finally, after months of reasoning and thinking, surrendered his life to Jesus. The great realisation came to him that no matter how ingenious and powerful the rockets he could design, they could only take him from this natural earth to the natural moon. What he needed was a spiritual power to take him from the natural earth to a spiritual heaven. This power was faith. He also realised that the growth and development needed in him to let go of all his knowledge and human abilities and to completely trust Jesus, was far greater than all the abilities of the scientific and engineering teams combined.

Hebrews 12:2 and 3 say that Jesus went through the most severe testing and after enduring pain and suffering, opposition and humiliation, He persisted and was glorified to sit on a throne next to His Father. When looking at Scripture and the champions of our faith, we cannot ignore a glaring reality. Whether we look at Paul, Jeremiah who suffered greatly, Job or many others, we see them walking out their faith amid great pressure.

I dare say a person who lives a comfortable and easy life doesn't find it necessary to live by faith (Romans 1:17). That person hasn't engaged the enemy and hasn't yet stepped into the realm of the spirit; all they've done is use their own natural talents and abilities. If we were able to live lives of worldly ease, we would not have entered a life of faith. The moment we step out of the boat and face a storm, it's at that moment that we need the gift of faith from the Spirit of Christ.

I can personally testify to the fact that my faith has developed greatly during testing times. It's often when a believer reaches the end of their ability to control a situation that faith begins to change it. By getting to the end of your own wisdom, resources and experience, you step into the realm of the spirit, and this normally takes place when you're engaging the enemy.

When we walk in God's will for our lives, we're almost always resisting the flesh, taking territory from the enemy, getting people saved and swimming upstream. Jesus said that we will have opposition in this life (John 16:33). The world hated Him and so would they hate us (John 15:18). Pressure draws us closer to God in the same way that fasting gets our body's attention. Saying no to food is a way to put the flesh second in line to the spirit. Pressure or testing forces us to decide to trust and obey God. It purifies us from doubt and double-mindedness. It takes our eyes off our personal abilities and we look to God to carry us.

When we undergo severe testing, our focus and values change from earthly to heavenly perspectives. We begin to understand why Jesus said His home and kingdom are not on earth. He knew very well what future torment awaited Him and this made Him rely more on His Father. True faith enables us to rely more on God than ourselves and our lives become more aligned to God's will and ways.

Chapter 19

God's command about routine

One of the great commands God gave Israel is to keep certain daily routines. Not only do routines keep a believer focused on God, they also ensure the person walks in a constant awareness of God's presence in and with them.

When functioning under severe pressure, there is an excellent tool available to us all – free and easily obtainable. This tool is to maintain a strong daily routine. It keeps the mind focused and healthy. Many people refer to them as habits, but that can have negative connotations as often people place their hope in human habits, which are doomed from the start. But those who have been under severe pressure while being wrongfully imprisoned have managed to keep their minds active and balanced by following strict daily routines. Israel's journey through the Wilderness for forty years is a good example of a group of people who followed daily routines given to them by God. These routines are not always spiritual, but they help believers maintain their spiritual health.

Sticking to a daily routine was a lifesaver for Daniel, a well-known Biblical figure. Daniel 6:10 says that he prayed to God three times a day, every day. We can appreciate this action more when reading up about the predicament that Daniel and his three friends, Shadrach, Meshack and Abednego, found themselves in. They were among the Israelites who were exiled to Babylon and were forced to learn the local language, live in a foreign culture and worship foreign gods, something they obviously did not do. As a result, Daniel was thrown into the lion's den. How did Daniel maintain his faith that God would protect him from the hungry lions? Daniel's faith, during his time working in King Darius's palace, was kept strong because of his daily routine of prayer and worship.

Our natural bodies depend on the correct daily nutritional intake to function optimally and so does our spiritual body. We need the correct intake to ensure we stand strong in the faith. This is true especially when we're under pressure for our faith. Pressure doesn't always signal the enemy's involvement. Scripture is clear that pressure purifies our faith and, in many instances, it's God who allows us to experience difficulty. Note what happened in Job's life when God allowed him to experience terrible suffering to prove his faith in God.

When we as believers train ourselves to maintain daily routines, we grow stronger in our resolve to trust God. When we do encounter difficulties, we do what we've done in the past – we call on the Lord for help. Having these daily routines and seeing how God has come through for us in the past, is another element of strength during the testing of our faith. Positive past experiences have a profound effect on our mindset when under pressure.

In the past, routines taught us to get on our knees, to read the Word of God and pray. When we did this, we saw results. These routines keep us in tune with God and what His Word teaches us.

Let's look at the flipside of the principle of maintaining healthy daily routines. Believers who have not instituted daily spiritual routine in their lives are easily uprooted by waves of testing. They begin to grab at straws and in sheer desperation, they begin to pray and claim Scripture verses. In most case, random acts like this don't show much fruit. God doesn't wat to be our fire insurance. He wants us to abide in Him and Him in us. He wants us to develop a relationship of trust with Him and the only way to do so is to commune with Him daily by reading His Word and praying.

The Apostle John was sent into exile and hard labour on the island of Patmos (Revelation 1:9). While living in harsh conditions he was in the Spirit (Revelation 1:10). Even while being imprisoned like a criminal by the Romans for sharing the Word of God and the testimony of Jesus, John did not forgo his daily routines. He remembered the Lord's Day, which shows us that he remembered how to remain connected to God. His spirit was linked to God's Spirit of revelation. Despite the testing circumstances he was forced into, John remained steadfast that nothing would cause his faith to stumble. Despite his age and circumstances, John's mind was clear when he penned the introduction in chapter 1. It's evident when he mentions "patient endurance" in verse nine, that to endure unwarranted punishment, he had to maintain a sound mind.

Why Lord?

Because we don't see the process from beginning to end and we experience it as it unfolds without any control over the situation, maintaining trust in God is a critical aspect of Christian living. The very foundation of trust is to relinquish control and to place your life in the hands of someone else.

Scripture makes is clear that faith is a process of development during which we undergo pressure, which purifies our faith. Why does our faith need purification? Looking back at the Garden of Eden, the devil's main objective was to destroy the relationship between humanity and God. He did this by focusing on the potential ability of humanity to be their own master. Adam and Eve failed in their attempt and were banished from God's presence. Their desire for self-rule was their sin. To this day, people still struggle with relinquishing control and allowing the Spirit of God to lead them.

> Since we live by the Spirit, let us keep in step with the Spirit. Galatians 5:25 (NIV)

It takes a total rebirth on the inside for a believer to allow the Spirit to lead them. A new believer must be born of the Spirit to be able hear and respond to the Spirit, which is followed by a process of renewing of their minds to abandon the sinful human nature and develop the mind of Christ (1 Corinthians 2:16).

It is not unusual for a believer to ask, "Why Lord?" in testing times. The purification process of a believer's faith can cause suffering and anguish, even to the point of death. This is because only God sees the outcome of our faith and it is His prerogative to mature and purify us.

This reminds me of a story I heard many years ago and that help me to keep going, even when things seem unfair and unjust. The story is about an old missionary flying back to his home country after serving a church in a foreign country for many years. The aged man had retired from actively serving the church where he and his late wife were missionaries. As he boarded the plane, he realised that a celebrity was also on the flight and when the time came for them to disembark, the passengers were asked to wait until the celebrity had disembarked. A large crowd of welcoming fans awaited the celebrity. Eventually the retired missionary was allowed to disembark and as he walked down the steps there was no one to welcome him home after so many years of serving the church. In his heart he asked God why he didn't have a welcome home. He felt God responding: "But, you are not home yet." This reply, which the man heard in his heart, settled everything instantly and it has done the same for me and many other believers. When we go through tough times and we have the urge to ask: "Why Lord?" we need to have the understanding that we are not living for this life. Our time here is not spent gathering wealth and wasting time and energy on things that are worthless and fruitless; we need to see beyond this life and into the life to come. The great multitude of witnesses mentioned in Hebrews 11 are cheering us on to run our race to the end and not lose hope.

When life seems unfair

I wish to relate a story that helped me keep going, even when things seem unfair. It's a story that helps the faithful see beyond the hill. The devil targets those who put their trust in God. He's not really bothered about the unsaved because they're under his control anyway.

The story is about an old man on an airplane flying back to his home country, having retired after serving as a missionary in a foreign country. It so happened that a celebrity was also on the flight and when the time came for them to disembark, the missionary and all the passengers were asked to wait until the celebrity disembarked. Outside, a crowd of fans awaited the celebrity.

The retired missionary was eventually allowed to disembark and as he walked down the steps there was no one to welcome him back home after so many years of serving the church. In his heart he asked God why he did not have a welcome home. He felt God respond by saying: "But, you're not home yet." This reply, which the man heard in his heart, settled everything instantly. It has done the same for me and for many other believers. When we go through tough times and we have the urge to ask, "why Lord?" we need to understand that we're not living for this life. Our time here is not spent gathering wealth and wasting time and energy on things that are worthless and fruitless. We need to see beyond this life and into the life to come. The great multitude of witnesses mentioned in Hebrews 11 are cheering us on to run our race to the end and not lose hope.

It's not surprising that to see that even Jesus in His last agonising moments on the cross asked a similar question. Jesus expresses his faith in His Father when He asked God why He was cut off from His presence (Matthew 27:46). Jesus held on to the trust He had in His Father to raise Him from the dead. Trust is challenged the moment a person cannot see what lies behind the curtain. It's as if we experience a void of God's presence, as if we find ourselves alone in the battle, and we begin to question why God would allow us to be tested. We feel exposed and alone in our mind battles as we try to maintain our trust in God.

How do we overcome the "Why Lord?" question that builds up in our minds and hearts? One of the best ways to buffer the thoughts of uncertainty is to follow the steps God Himself gave to Israel. He asked them this paraphrased question: Have I not always looked after you, protected you and provided for you in the past?

Be aware of the great cloud of witnesses who remained faithful in trusting God through their suffering. Can so many believers who put their trust in God over millennia be wrong? If we as fathers treat our children with the greatest care and love, is this not a reflection of how the Father treats us?

The value of resistance

Resistance reveals the true state of a person's mind. Whether they resist negativity in the natural or in the spiritual, it means they stay true to a prescribed set of rules or values. Resistance is a tough process, but it also comes with great rewards. Resistance means investing the time and energy to focus on a single purpose; it requires knowledge about what is true and the ability to spot a fake.

Resistance is the second step in the process of purification. The first step is undergoing some sort of test. God allows scenarios and events to take place in our lives to evaluate our faith. It's not because He's unsure about our commitment to Him, but because He wants us to see our need for purification. Once we understand that we need help to be purified, we see our need to develop into a new person who obeys God. Testing helps us see where we're weak and vulnerable. The reason that people fail when tested is because they're not prepared in the time of testing and ignorance of the enemy's strategies allows a person to be easily overcome.

On a sports field, the ignorant person may underestimate their opposition and be easily intimidated by the noise.

Sports people understand the need for resistance. A runner who runs with weights becomes stronger. A bodybuilder who resists fast food understands the need for a healthy diet. Without resisting the unclean, a person can never be pure. Resistance removes what is impure.

Before salvation, people had been walking in a direction set by their fleshly wisdom and desires. When salvation enters the person's heart, they begin to see what God desires for them and whatever is outside God's plan will resist the Spirit of God within them.

Hebrews 12:2,3 say it is God who purifies our faith. He is the origin of our faith and the One who will perfect it. How does He perfect it? He allows events into our lives to challenge us to show us the value of resistance.

Resisting not only sets us free, it keeps us free. At the point of salvation, the enemy will bring fear and distraction to prevent the person from being made new on the inside. Later, the believer must resist the temptations to sin to maintain their relationship with God. Not resisting sin will cause them to fall back into a life of brokenness and weakness.

A person will often look for a helping hand, but not every hand is the hand of God. How then do we resist the hand that is not God's? How do we discern which is the right hand to take? We do this by educating ourselves on the Word of God. Faith is deposited into our hearts when hearing the Word of God; it's what births and develops our faith and illuminates our minds and hearts to what God desires.

Once we begin to understand the nature and mind of God from Scripture, we see how it's opposed to the wisdom, the ways and the pursuits of the world. Once our minds and hearts have been illuminated to know God's ways, we begin to experience a great battle within us. This is the battle of the Spirit resisting the flesh and this is the reason Jesus suffered on the cross. He came to take away our sin, which is why we have to resist what is not of God.

Resistance, as Hebrews explains, begins small, but it will be like Jesus' journey. Biblical resistance is a process of crucifixion of the old person. It's a brutal fight against what leads to eternal death. Resistance is the agent that purifies our motives and affects our actions. For a person to say no to something, they first need to investigate what is being offered and secondly what the effects would be if the offer is accepted.

Resistance in a believer's life comes when the person trusts the Word of God. We've been given God's will for us and the way to walk in it. We've been given the history of Israel and the events of the early church to understand what to do and what not to do. The Word of God is full of insight, teachings and stories of people's lives who either resisted the enemy's advances and those who fell away eternally because they did not resist the enemy.

Chapter 20

Faith and people's values

T he lives of unsaved people all tend to exhibit the same traits. Their decisions are made by themselves and for themselves, based on their own set of rules and values. But who validates if they're right in what they say, believe and do? Is there a universal set of rules and values that apply to all of humanity? Yes, indeed there is. All of us were at one point fully in charge of our own lives and followed our own ideas, living according to our self-constructed ideologies – at least, so we thought. Unbelievers live by the values they grew up with and the experiential knowledge they gathered along the way. Unbelievers are their own blind guides and they judge themselves according to their own best efforts.

Faith, on the other hand, is a principle of trusting God and placing your hope in His universal set of rules and values. Faith is letting go of your values and embracing God's. By doing so, you effectively give God full control of your live, your destiny and your problems. This is exactly what takes place the moment that an unbeliever hands over control of their lives and embraces God's gift of eternal life. It is easier said than done, because to hand over control to God is not easy at all. That's why God says in Hebrews 11:6 that we must first believe that He exists when we approach Him for help.

The problem that we as believers have when it comes to trusting in something or someone is that we're inclined to follow our own ideas, values and rules because of how we grew up as unbelievers. Before salvation, we were our own judge and jury and we judged ourselves based on our own values and not on the Word of God. But our values are subjective collections of random ideas compared with God's Word.

This also makes it easy for people to forgive themselves when they do something wrong – because they live by their own standards, they can amend them when needed, especially in the face of scientific advances and increasing knowledge. However, when people are introduced to the Word of Truth, they suddenly realise they're in trouble. They are confronted with the universal objective truth and not their own subjective values.

In the Garden of Eden, Satan convinced Adam and Eve that they could be like God (Genesis 3:5). He proposed a set of ever-changing subjective rules that allowed them to decide their own fate and future, which included a way to decide how to judge themselves in the case of an error, based on their own values. All of this was done to eliminate punishment for sin. The problem with subjective values is that people cannot be their own judge and jury when deciding on punishment for their own volitional mistakes.

Faith in God's Word

Faith in God's Word is the beginning of a person's punishment for their sin. First, God's Word finds humanity guilty of sin and second, God's Word proclaims the way to freedom from sin. Both are needed because the guilty verdict and the proclamation of forgiveness and freedom are external to humanity. Both are from God who declares people guilty and forgives us. Both are done by God and both require faith – the spiritual gift from God. Initially, the Spirit allows the person to understand their sin and then the Spirit provides the gift of faith, which enables the person to trust God for salvation.

Faith does not allow a person to base their hope on their own set of values. Faith begins with and is a gift from God. Only reliance on and obedience to God's Word will result in faith being answered by God. People cannot negotiate with God on what constitutes faith. This means that we cannot expect God to supernaturally supply what we need if we follow our own subjective guidelines. If this were the case, then Ephesians 2:8-9, which negates people's achievements in the supernatural realm, is false. The fall of humanity in the garden was the result of their belief that they could trust their own judgement and ignore God's guidelines and commands.

Romans 10:17 says that an eternal and supernatural change takes place in a person's life when they hear the Word of God for salvation and thereafter for sanctification. This is the point when subjectivity is replaced by objectivity; when truth enters to solidify and secure a person's hope. Only God's Word can be an anchor because God's Word is unchangeable and represents His pure infallible nature. His Word never changes.

Looking for scorpions

As a young boy, my friends and I used to venture into the mountain behind our home looking for scorpions. We knew that these little critters were found only underneath rocks, so we looked for an area where there were lots of rocks. We began turning over every rock to see what we could find. We were careful not to put our fingers underneath the rocks because the scorpions we were looking for could give a nasty sting. Instead, we used our shoes to lift the rocks and look underneath for the scorpions. These arachnids lived in the cool dark areas underneath the rocks, well-hidden from view and they didn't like being exposed. They are masters of disguise and if provoked, as small as they are, they put up a big show of force.

One of the so-called "unpleasant" aspects of faith – at least to the flesh – is the waiting game. While waiting on God to deliver what we need, an interesting process starts to unfold. A multitude of factors develop during this process, from stormy emotions to disbelief, taking charge of the situation and having a short temper, to anger with God, questioning one's faith and more.

Interestingly, each person has a different "scorpion" under their rock. One believer might resent God's silence, another questions God's Word, while another works on Plan B. It's often here that God begins to overturn every rock in our lives to reveal what's hidden beneath. He does so for our own sake – the scorpions under our rocks refer to hidden things we might not be aware of. The process God begins is similar for every believer but its outworking is person-specific. Every person has a weakness and when it comes to faith and this weakness is amplified. Often the amplification is in the area where the believer struggles. God will overturn every rock in our lives until He reveals the scorpion, the weakness we have that hinders the growth of our faith.

God will not leave a single stone unturned. He will push into our lives and lift every area of our lives until our weaknesses and vices are exposed and removed. He will not leave us the same as we were before He found us. This is the exact reason we are to walk by faith. For one person, their weakness might be food, for another a hidden explosive temper, yet another person may not like confronting the enemy and they easily give up the fight. Some peoples' emotions lead them in winding meanders of uncertainty and doubt, while others merely believe God will do as He pleases anyway. For instance, when the Old Testament Israelites journeyed through the Wilderness, they made food and water their main source of complaint against Moses and God.

For someone who grew up in a broken home, trust will be an area they will need to work hard at. Eating disorders, excessive exercise and future-anxiety are some of the scorpions hiding under people's rocks. No person is the same, and therefore the tests they will face will be unique to their personality, upbringing, life experience and character. God allows these tests to drill down deep into the person's subconscious, to the root of their weakness. He will construct scenarios from which we cannot escape. The believer who walks by faith will see many scorpions come out from underneath rocks in their lives. These scorpions do not surprise God. Rather, it pleases Him to see that people are being set free and transformed. Liberating change comes when secrets are exposed and addressed. Is it pleasant to have your rocks turned over? Definitely not, but there is a freedom that comes to the believer that enhances their faith in the whole process.

The dominant realm in my life

I have often asked myself if Peter, John and Paul had more of God's Spirit than we do? They performed great miracles and seemed to have had the faith to heal the sick. Their remarkable exploits are documented where they spoke to kings and prominent people. They never operated in fear during these events. Did they have more of the Spirit than you and me, or did the Spirit have more of them than He has of you and me? This is from one of Dr RT Kendall's teachings.

When our focus is more on the Spirit and the life to come, then something of what Peter, John and Paul had or did becomes noticeable. They all endured severe trials for Jesus' sake and from their lives it becomes clear that they lost the desire for anything in this world; their focus was the Gospel, the glory of God and the world to come.

In the discussion about looking for scorpions, I mentioned the effort God goes to in the life of every person who wants to walk by faith, to empty them of any worldly desires or of any hooks the world has in their flesh. By looking at the lives of the three men, Peter, John and Paul, we see that nothing this world could offer interested them. Paul even says that he had counted anything in this world as loss compared to the surpassing worth of knowing Christ as Lord. He said that for Jesus' sake he had lost all things.

> What is more, I consider everything a loss because of the surpassing worth of knowing Christ Jesus my Lord, for whose sake I have lost all things. I consider them garbage, that I may gain Christ and be found in him, not having a righteousness of my own that comes from the law, but that which is through faith in Christ—the righteousness that

comes from God on the basis of faith. Philippians
3:8,9 (NIV)

From the lives of the three men mentioned above, I want to
suggest that the extent of their death to this world had a direct
bearing on their success in their faith. To the measure they walked
away from the desires, pleasures and lures of this world, to the
same measure they succeeded in changing the natural by means
of the supernatural. They made faith and the spiritual world it
operates in, the dominant realm in their lives. To achieve this is no
small task. It tends to happens through severe persecution and
hardship. Is this not what James 1:2-4 says? The testing of your
faith brings perseverance, which produces perfection and
completeness in the believer so that they lack nothing? The more
intense the persecution, the greater the development of the
person's faith and the greater their reward.

Lastly, there is another benefit we see in the lives of these three
men who walked by faith and who experienced tremendous persecution. Making the realm of the Spirit their dominant realm
allowed for a tremendous depth of growth. In the first verses of
Revelation 1 it is evident that the Apostle John is suffering in
custody for the sake of the Word (Revelation 1:9). He was willing
to sacrifice everything and the result was that he wrote one of the
most astounding prophecies in Scripture that depicts great
revelation.

The Apostle Paul had the experience of being caught up into the
third heaven (2 Corinthians 12) at a vulnerable time in his life. He
suffered persecution, he was dealing with a struggling church in
Corinth, and he was given a mysterious thorn in the flesh to keep
him reliant on God. Paul had seen things in the third heaven that
human minds cannot fathom or describe in words. His level of

revelation was incredible yet God kept him reliant on Him for the duration of his life on earth. This reliance, also understood as a brokenness, is what allows faith to work. It symbolises a total loss of earthly concerns and total reliance on God. This is what made men like Peter, John and Paul such powerful men in the Spirit.

What would life be like for the believer if there was no testing or persecution? The answer is another question: what is the benefit of testing or persecution? Without testing or persecution we cannot grow and develop. Think about it. If God allows testing and persecution, it must have a purpose. The result of testing and persecution is that it leads to steadfastness, resilience and character development and we are perfected, established and strengthened.

Chapter 21

Waiting and worshipping

W e cannot speak about faith without mentioning the human part of it. Although faith is a spiritual gift from the Spirit of God deposited into the heart of a person, the reality of the human mind still exists. Faith as a spiritual act opposes the mind of the person who's operating in faith. Faith and trust are used interchangeably by Jesus – and trusting God means not trusting your own devices and abilities.

The process of trusting God for something we need has three stages, as explained earlier in this book.

The initial "walking on water" stage is the decision to not look at the challenges in front of us. These challenges could be the many obstacles we might stumble over or the void of anything to hold onto. Both are a major challenge to our human minds because we prefer something we can see, touch and feel because in them lie the safety and security we as frail humans so desperately desire. The disciple called Thomas made this very clear when he said that seeing is believing (John 20:25).

The second stage is the toughest stage; this is the time in between asking and receiving. It's the waiting stage where we cannot see the result of our faith yet we're taught to focus our hope on God's faithfulness. The human mind is blindsided by faith here because faith doesn't make sense when we want to rely on human reason, which says, "Get out there and do it yourself. Why not skip the waiting stage and force the end to come?" This was one of Jesus' greatest tests on the cross. Perhaps, in the moment of tremendous anguish and suffering, Jesus mind was telling him: "Take charge of the situation because your Father has abandoned you. Call on the angels and climb down from the cross." To some extent it's easy to take the decision to trust God, but it might not be so easy to maintain that trust during severe internal and external pressure.

John Lennox, the Irish Christian apologist, once said that faith is not hope in the absence of truth, which some call "blind faith." Faith is guided by three key elements. First, the immutable, inerrant and eternal Word of God that teaches us about faith and instructs us to rely on God. Second, our faith is bolstered by accounts in Scripture where God has shown His faithfulness to those who put their trust in Him. Third, our personal accounts where God has carried us in the past are powerful testimonies that we can put our faith in Him.

To walk on water, a believer must first learn to walk by faith. They must equip themselves with the necessary skills to maintain their stand until God answers their prayer. It's one thing to take a particular position, but it's quite another to defend that position in the face of opposition.

To illustrate the principle of waiting for God to answer our prayers, the structure of a suspension bridge comes to mind. Both ends of a suspension bridge are secure. However, the moment someone decides to leave one side and walk across is when everything begins to feel unstable and unsure. This is the time when doubts, anxiety, fear and unbelief begin to captivate the mind. Interestingly, even though the suspension bridge has been in place for a long time, the person crossing it will be flooded with thoughts of it breaking. It's during this time of uncertainty that the believer needs to practice "active waiting". Faith is active not passive. It's similar to a farmer sowing seed and then regularly watering the seed. But until the harvest comes, faith requires an active standing over the seeds by the farmer.

What is active waiting then? There are many examples in Scripture of people placing their trust in God and expecting a breakthrough. In most cases, the individuals or groups had to spend time waiting for God to deliver what they requested. Trusting in God or living by faith has its challenges. The greatest challenge is the carnal mind that we as believers must overcome. Our minds aren't regenerated the moment we are justified, as some people expect. We live our entire lives fighting against the carnality that we were born with. It's our old sinful distrusting nature that poses the greatest challenge to trusting God fully.

Waypoints in the process

When we dissect the journey of trusting God for something we need, we see several waypoints emerge in the process. We begin by trusting God for who He is and that He rewards those who diligently seek Him. Then we verbalise our need to Him, and at this point our request remains with God until He fulfils it. This time of waiting becomes a warzone in our minds. Questions pop into our minds questioning God's genuineness, His ability and willingness to help, and our mistakes that could preclude us from receiving. Our thoughts play see-saw with us and one moment we feel positive, the next we feel negative. Our minds treat every thought as a court proceeding where the possible outcome of our request is argued. Here the devil can play havoc with our emotions and where he could cause us to lose faith in God – all because of a delay in His answer. We must agree that the carnal flesh doesn't want to die without a fight. In sin we were born and our old nature distrust of God. It takes time to trust God, not because He has a questionable track record, but because we were His former enemies. We sinned and lost the glory He destined us for and we violated His trust. Our natures had to be reborn to begin to trust God. We had to give Him control of our lives and allow Him to direct our steps.

Allowing the mind to passively wait for God's answer is a risky endeavour. We need to busy ourselves with something while we wait for God to deliver His answer. We must take up something constructive while we wage war against the thoughts of disbelief the devil sends our way. A passive mind is a fertile ground for seeds of unbelief and instead of guarding our minds, we allow the enemy to sow seeds of confusion.

As these seeds begin to sprout, fruit of disbelief begin to grow – and that's the enemy's strategy. He patiently erodes our faith in God by defeating us in our minds. Waiting on God is not enough. The wise believer busies themself with worshipping God. This can take many forms and is not necessarily sitting in a church pew singing Hymns and Psalms. It can be active as we serve God and His church in many ways. It can be said that a busy person doesn't have time to sit and dwell on negativity.

There were people like Elijah who opposed the Baal worship; or the apostles who waited for the Spirit in the upper room; and there was Abraham, who prepared the sacrifice God requested and then had to wait for God to appear.

Waiting and worshipping

Waiting and worshipping work together. Only waiting exposes the mind to seeds of doubt and negativity and only worshipping can make the believer become impatient and question why God doesn't hear them. A high-functioning person with an active problem-solving mind will find it rather hard to both wait and worship because they're used to taking charge and getting the job done. It will require a systematic "letting go" by the person to let God do what they've asked Him to. In many cases a person with an active mind will experience longer delays as they take more time to surrender their own will to God. By both waiting and worshipping, the believer allows God to show His deliverance, anchoring their faith in God. A person who's waiting for God to answer their request must keep their minds active because the devil will pound their mind with negative thoughts. An active mind is not idle; it remains alert and ready to act against any negative thoughts from the enemy.

Does faith require my inactivity?

Sitting idle when waiting for God to move in my situation is not something I see in Scripture. Faith is not a passive principle. What we see when we study the history and journey of Israel in Scripture is the promise God made to Israel. He promised them a land of their own and that He would dwell there with them. He promised to be with them, provide for them, fight for them and more. At the same time, Israel was not required to passively sit by and wait for God to deliver their inheritance; they were to be actively engaged in taking their inheritance. They had to engage the enemy, stand up and fight and take charge.

Israel sent out spies to research the enemy's capabilities, the weapon they had at their disposal, their strategies, the condition and number of their fighting men, and the logistics of the city walls they were to take. Being shepherds, they had to ensure the land they were going to could provide enough grazing. They also had to establish if the land had plenty of wood to build houses and other structures.

Taking Jericho required that Israel march around the city for seven days until God stepped in. He didn't act until the nation fulfilled what God had commanded them to do. Receiving their promises came when Israel actively participated. Trusting God for their promises was, as Scripture reveals, not a passive exercise.

Practically speaking, let me share steps in a journey we as a family had to walk to reach where we are now serving in the church. One night I had a dream that had several segments of a long journey. I found it encouraging that the dream was not a total surprise to me and it confirmed what I had been feeling in my heart for many years. In the dream I saw a distant geographical place. There were some hints and familiar landmarks to help me where my investigation should start. While investigating the dream and the location where we were to go, other voices and hints became clear. But sticking to the dream gave me great peace and assurance. I looked for more detail as I tried to put together some ways to help me find our destiny and where our future place of service would be. The dream did not have a voice outright telling me where, when and who.

Amazingly, it was the day that I got into my car and drove to where I felt I was led that the details became a lot clearer. Suddenly the bigger picture was in front of me and I began recognising the landmarks and familiar surroundings. The direction towards our next destination felt right. In the area where I stopped, I met some people; I joined a place where there were church meetings; I made enquiries; I made calls; I visited congregations; I met more people; I answered many questions. I knocked on several doors but only a few opened.

Some things took me by surprise because in my limited understanding I interpreted some details in the dream incorrectly. I wasn't walking blind nor was I trying to make things work. I learnt to be patient and wait for the Spirit to confirm what I had seen in the dream.

Was everything clear at the start; did I have all the answers? The answer is no. Some of the people I met who walked with me initially were not there after a while and some who were there at are still with me. While actively investigating the area, it felt as if a narrowing down of options, people and venues was taking place. It was by no means a passive journey. It was a spying out of the land; making enquiries and discussing with authorities, but as we put one foot in front of the other, God's plan was taking shape. Looking back now, what we are doing seems like the obvious thing, but when we set out in faith, the route was not so obvious. Also, if we were passive and just waited for the dream to materialise, I am confident that we would not have arrived at our God-intended destination for this season.

Chapter 22

Can God agree to our all requests?

A s a pastor I'm often asked about faith. Recently a believer asked: "Why doesn't God answer my prayer? I've been waiting for months and had no answer yet." Often, when prayer requests are made to God and aren't answered, we need to look at what was asked. People sometimes have requests in their hearts that God cannot grant. It goes back to an example of two boxers in the ring. Both asked God to grant them the win but who does God answer?

Delays can also stem from haphazard or ignorant requests made by believers, which God cannot grant. Another example is when people pray sincerely to God for the lotto numbers. They even put their faith in action and with great expectation they begin to wait on God for the winning numbers. In their heats they are genuinely practicing their faith. We call such efforts: "Righteous gains through unrighteous means." God will never allow it or answer such a request. All the believer will receive for their efforts is a very delayed answer from God.

True faith requires the believer's total surrender of their efforts, talents, resources and abilities, and that what they're asking God for is in line with the plan He has for their lives. A total surrender is an inward laying down of my will to see my requests fulfilled. I have to trust God to hear and grant my request and I also have to ensure my request falls within His will. If a believer refuses to surrender their prayer requests to God's scrutiny, there's no need for Him to grant the request. It is one of the hardest things for a believer to do, to surrender their request before God before even making the request. Believers are quick to pray, "If it is your will," but sometimes this prayer is followed up by claiming whatever they prayed for in faith. The request and the claim for an answered prayer cannot be in the same sentence.

How can we identify a prayer request that will not be answered? We need to look for a request that has not first been submitted to God. When these requests remain unanswered and the person's expectation remains unfulfilled, anger can set in and questions asked: "Why has God done this to me? Does He not love me, or am I being punished for something I did wrong?" How the person handles rejection when asking for things God cannot grant is a good indicator of whether they surrendered their request before God for approval. Knowing God's will regarding our requests, or at least trying to pursue what He wants for us, is important in God's eyes and it is how we can be sure our requests will be answered.

When God steps in

Faith is expressed when someone puts their trust in God. It might start off as partial trust, but God desires this trust to become a complete reliance on Him. Scripture is clear that a person who decides to walk by faith will attract the enemy's attention (Job 1:8-11 and Revelation 12:17) and there are many Scripture verses available to the believer to withstand the enemy's attacks. The deep-rooted relational trust that God's children place in Him is a key focus for the enemy. Genesis 3:1-5 shows how the serpent targeted the relationship Adam and Eve had with God. Satan is envious of this relationship and will do his best to derail it.

A believer who steps out of their boat to walk on water attracts the attention of God and the enemy. Hebrews 11:6 says that God rewards the believer who walks by faith and His purpose is to develop the believer. The enemy's sole purpose is to drive them away from God and destroy them.

I want to focus on the role God plays in the development of the believer during the phase when the believer puts their trust in God. Few principles are as honouring to someone when a person places their complete trust in them. It's an expression of love that few other actions can match. The aim of the Gospel is to develop relational trust between God and the believer. God wants to be their provider, protector and sustainer and He wants them to trust Him completely as Jesus did in His final utterance on the cross (Luke 23:46).

Part of the process to develop trust is when God does something many believers and unbelievers might misunderstand. God tests the believer's resolve by not intervening when called upon and during the testing, a believer might question God and feel as if God has abandoned them.

A key aspect to be remembered is that testing can only come to a believer during a faith trial that God has allowed and is according to His will. This means it will ultimately be for the good of the believer (1 Peter 1:6,7).

In all this you greatly rejoice, though now for a little
while you may have had to suffer grief in all kinds of
trials. These have come so that the proven genuineness
of your faith—of greater worth than gold, which
perishes even though refined by fire—may result in
praise, glory and honour when Jesus Christ is revealed.
(NIV)

Make no mistake, God never abandons the believer. Even though
their lives on earth might end, His rewards in the life to come for
placing your trust in Him are beyond words. When God begins
the process of transforming a person's trust in Him, He sets out to
transform baby faith into mature faith. In this process He might
sometimes prevent certain tools that are available to the believer
from being effective in driving the enemy away. Examples include
Paul being unable to drive away the messenger of Satan, the
thorn in his flesh, which God allowed (2 Corinthians 12:7); Jesus
could have defended Himself from the suffering on the cross by
calling on legions of angels to defend and destroy His enemies
(Matthew 26:53). All the apostles apart from John died as martyrs
for the Gospel. God did not prevent Paul's harsh imprisonments
nor did He stop the beheading of John the Baptist (Matthew
14:10).

Trust is only as strong as when it is truly tested and throughout
history even the giants of faith have been tested. In the process of
testing, God audits the believer's faith and He assesses it to expose
any self-reliance, which is false faith. God exposes false faith
because the believer will suffer great loss if this is all they rely on
and it shows the believer the areas they need to work on in their
spiritual lives. Testing a believer's faith to extreme will reveal if
their trust is truly in God.

Here's an illustration about trusting God that I was given in my younger days in Sunday School. Imagine a man about to be crucified. Both feet and arms need to be secured to the wooden cross. If the guard handed the hammer and metal spikes to the man who's being crucified to pin himself down, will he not have second thoughts? Will he not try to postpone the process, pull out the metal spikes and refuse the process from being completed? When we trust God, we must allow Him to bring our self-reliance to an end. We need to hand Him the hammer to complete the process of trusting Him completely. This is the reason we celebrate water baptism; it signifies the old self being crucified and the new person rising to walk with God, fully relying on Him. No believer can mature in their faith when self-reliance is still a tool they employ to bring about God's purposes.

Psalm 50:15 says we are to call on God in the day of trouble and He will deliver us. Scripture also says that God gave Paul a thorn in his flesh, which Paul himself could not set himself free from. No matter the amount of spiritual warfare and resistance Paul engaged in, commanding it to flee, God allowed this situation to persist. In 2 Corinthians 12:7-10 Paul sad it made his self-reliance weaker so that his reliance on God could be stronger. His weakness made him more dependent on God and less dependent on himself.

By laying down our abilities and simply trusting in God might seem to be a sign of weakness, but when we let go of self-reliance, God steps in powerfully. One of the reasons Paul had to learn to be fully dependent on God and not on himself is the reason that so many great men and women of God have fallen throughout history. They begin to walk in self-reliance. The flesh cannot achieve anything in God's eyes and relying on it gives the enemy one of his greatest weapons. Self-reliance can also be expressed as weakness, while relying on God is strength. The enemy will search until he finds a particular situation related to the person's weaknesses, and he will bring them down. The flesh, no matter how powerful it might appear, is powerless against the pursuit of a spiritual enemy.

Faith's supernatural results

Faith is a spiritual force that enables the believer to live in this natural world using supernatural means. When believers start to see supernatural results and they begin developing divine insights, the enemy will be knocking at their door. It is for this reason that God steps in to end the boastfulness of the flesh. He will postpone the believer's breakthrough and allow testing to pursue to believer. He will keep the believer under His hand until all reliance on the flesh has been depleted. It's better to be in the hand of a loving Father who wants the best for his children, than living a life of ignorance that's governed by self-reliance. This way, God receives the glory and not any believer.

The risk associated with great revelation is the elevation of the flesh and the downfall of the person. God steps in to assure great revelation is balanced with great purification, working towards great rewards for the person. Philippians 1:6 says God, who began the process of the good work in you, will complete the process of transforming the believer. This process often sees God as a loving Father stepping in to develop the believer in many ways.

Stepping over the threshold

Delays in answered prayer is a principle all believers must deal with. Believers often grow weary after a long period of waiting for

God to answer their prayers. The mind can be a painful master as it often constructs many scenarios about why God is not answering the prayer. Perhaps the person feels unworthy, not good enough, perhaps they think they're not praying enough or in the wrong manner. Some believers have given prayer and faith a try, just to decide after a while to go it alone. When frustration sets in, so does anger and resentment. We can be sure that God will never call us to a faith project that we cannot achieve. It is well and truly out of our grasp to achieve an outcome in any project God calls us to in our own strength. This is the essence of faith – to humble ourselves; to end all human efforts and wait for God to do the impossible.

An insightful Bible account about trusting God is when God called Abraham to take his son Isaac up Mount Moriah to sacrifice him as a burnt offering to God (Genesis 22:1 1-18). You can imagine the thought that must have run wild in Abraham's mind. If God promised him a son, then why was God asking him to sacrifice the promise? Genesis 22:2 makes this clear when God said: "Your only son, whom you love." What made it difficult for Abraham was that if he sacrificed Isaac, the promised nation of Israel was doomed before it started. Hebrews 11:19 says Abraham reasoned that even if he had sacrificed Isaac, God was able to bring him back from the dead. Although it seemed a barbaric act for a father to sacrifice his son, the people Abraham originated from were known to sacrifice children as part of their pagan beliefs and fertility rituals. However, they were not known for raising the dead.

The father and son walked up the mountain as planned, but everything was turned upside down when Isaac asked about the lamb for the sacrifice. Abraham told Isaac that God would supply the sacrifice (Genesis 22:8). The period between this question and the next event must have truly tested Abraham's mind. How will God fulfil the promise of a nation if He cannot bring the son of promise back to life?

It's important to remember that with every great step of faith, there must be a promise from God to hold onto. This is what kept Abraham walking up Mount Moriah, undeterred by Isaac's question. Abraham reasoned that if God promised a nation from his offspring, then God would have to start and complete the process. Abraham knew it was impossible for him and Sarah to "help God out" here. The Genesis 12:1-3 promise was what kept Abraham walking and not trying to find a way out in his own wisdom and strength.

What often happens in the lives of believers is that they try to create their own promises, but without a promise from God, no believer has no firm ground to stand on. All they can do is what Abraham did, which is to present their manmade project to God and see if He will bring it to life (Genesis 17:18).

When the promise is absent or unlawfully claimed, no matter how hard the believer might pray or petition God, He will not turn their dead works into living beings. If there is a promise, the believer can hold on until God answers their prayers. God cannot lie, and His promises are yes and amen in Christ.

The time in between

I firmly believe that we as believers have a part to play in the time between praying and receiving God's answer. We can affect how long it takes to receive God's answer. We have the key to the situation we are in. While it's true that in our own strength we cannot change natural things, we can move forward in receiving God's answer.

Most people will expect this key to be something we need to achieve, while in fact, it is not what people can achieve, but rather what they can let go of. Humanity needs to take their eyes off themselves, calm their mind and wait on God for the answer to His promise.

Allow me to explain from Scripture. In the account of Abraham walking up Mount Moriah to sacrifice his son, we see the principle that unlocks God's hand. Genesis 22:12 says: "Now I know that you fear God." This says that Abraham had to get to a place in his heart and mind where he had totally abandoned the possibility of withdrawing his trust in God or having a Plan B in his pocket. Abraham came to the end of his ideas, plans, internal debates and creative scheming. In his mind, he has already sacrificed Isaac and seen God bring him back to life. In Abraham's mind, he had seen the future – the promised nation of Israel living in the Promised Land. There was no doubt in Abraham, no uncertainty and no going back. It's at the point that Abraham declared all his plans and efforts as fruitless and he leaned on God's promise. He stepped over the natural threshold and into the realm of the supernatural. He left behind all human planning and received God's promise as if it was there in front of him. This is the moment when God sad: "Now I know" (Genesis 22:12). This was the moment that Abraham leapt headlong into God's arms, knowing that He who promised is faithful (Hebrews 11:11).

Trusting God to raise Isaac again after sacrificing him was not the first time Abraham had to step over the natural threshold and into the realm of the supernatural. He had done so when he trusted God for a son (Romans 4:21). Paul makes the following powerful statement regarding Abraham's frame of mind when he says Abraham was "fully persuaded" (Romans 4:21). When a believer has breached the natural threshold and experienced the supernatural realm once, it seems as if they can do so again with a sense of ease, as is the pattern we see in Abraham's life – from obeying God and leaving his father's house, departing for an unknown country, to trusting God to do the impossible to open Sarah's womb, to raising his son from the dead after he obediently sacrificed him.

What we learn from the principle of a natural threshold is that until we abandon all rights, claims and efforts, we will see the answers to our prayers being delayed. When we reach the threshold of "no turning back" we receive the key to unlock God's supernatural provision. To step over the threshold is to completely trust God unconditionally.

Chapter 23

Death brings life

Standing alongside death beds and conducting funerals teaches you one definite thing: death is final. It's a body of work, a personality, a start and a finish; it's a life reaching completion. Death is a statement that humanity is not in command and it reveals what humanity cannot change. Death is not the end of all things, but a bridge to something new. This bridge is beyond people's grasp, which is the reason Paul said in Romans 1:17 that the righteous shall live by faith. He meant that living by faith also refers to the transition from the natural life into the spiritual life through death. The faith the believer has developed during their life is the bridge that allows them to walk into eternal life.

I want to use death to explain an important principle about faith. If death depicts a finality, then faith is at work when death has done its work in the fleshly realm. Faith is the gift from God to empower a believer to do what God has called them to and what they cannot do in their own strength. For this to happen, death must come to all of humanity's efforts. Should a person be able to accomplish, in their own strength, what God has called them to then the person will rival God for the glory. Faith is a gift that levels the playing field and has no preferences when it comes to social standing, nor does it show any favouritism. It's for this reason that death – a metaphorical end – must come to a person's efforts to either empower or better themself.

Pure faith at work

Scripture reveals a surprising element in the lives of those who demonstrated or were part of an event where pure faith was at work. The following accounts show how believers who stood firm in their trust in God went through a metaphorical "funeral" to see their requests answered by God. In these examples, death to people's efforts brought life to God's plans.

- When Abraham was asked to sacrifice his son Isaac. In his mind, God would bring his son back from the dead.
- Peter's sinking when walking on water.
- Jonah in the belly of the giant fish.
- Hagar and Ishmael after being cast out.
- Believers in Hebrews 11 who embraced death, yet without seeing the promise fulfilled, they held onto God's Word.
- Elijah at Mt Carmel knowing that if God did not show up, he would be dead.

A reason for the season

By now you would have seen that faith attracts opposition from a few sources, generally three. One, our flesh, which is our inherited carnal nature and does not appreciate being bypassed and disciplined. Two, the devil, who would do everything in his power to get the believer not to trust God because trust is a crucial part of a relationship. Three, God's plan is for every believer is to approach Him in faith, which requires the believer to willingly set aside their own human plans, self-reliance and wisdom to see God's spiritual wisdom, His plans and His provision becoming active in the life of the believer.

God's invitation to believers to trust Him comes with a reward (Hebrews 11:6). God's plan comes with a season in which the believer will undergo rebirth. This process starts with justification, after which the newborn Christian must first crawl, then stumble and eventually walk in the spirit. This is the new life that God calls every believer to – and it's a process that God never bypasses. Part of the progression from spiritual infancy towards maturity will bring opposition, uncertainties, persecution, anger and possibly rebellion, as seen in the Israelites' confronting of Moses (Numbers 14:1-4).

Most of Paul's life, post-salvation, was spent in jail. During this time, he wrote many of the books in the New Testament. God's timing was not off because He had a specific purpose for Paul. While enduring daily persecution and life-threatening situations, God's wisdom was shown when He hid Paul in jail – safe from his adversaries. Was it unpleasant being locked up in jail? Undoubtedly it was, but the effect is that since that time, Paul's writings bring salvation to people every day.

The reason for the season is that you and I need to find out what God's plan for our lives is. Being kept in isolation or being persecuted are not always bad things. If it were, then Paul was not treated fairly by God. We need to understand that God used Paul, who was a skilled orator and a powerful teacher, to write God's message of love to the whole world. God called Paul, equipped him with the Gospel message and employed him to bless others. If Paul had been martyred prematurely, it's likely that many New Testament books would not have been written.

Time spent in tough circumstances and in obscurity when walking by faith is God's plan for the believer. His plan also includes His perfect timing. He planned Jesus' and Paul's lives to perfection. If Jesus had been pushed off the edge of the cliff by an angry mob (Luke 4:29), and Paul had been killed prematurely, then we have no hope. But God had already planned for His servants to spend time in obscurity when He would harness the talents, gifts and abilities He had given them before birth. The outworking of their time in God's service had a powerful effect on the communities of their time on earth, as well as on the past, present and future.

Small things carry weight

Often people want to be known for using their gifts. They expect a large public platform to draw greater reward from God. If they feel more important than others, they attach God's approval to their subjective feeling. This is not true at all. If Jesus said a glass of water given to a thirsty person will be blessed by Him, then the small things we do for everyday people around us carry weight before God (Matthew 10:40-42). Our Father in heaven, who sees everything done in secret, will reward every doer of such an act (Matthew 6:6-7). James says true religion is looking after widows and orphans and in God's eyes, this act draws His attention (James 1:27).

The next time you find yourself in a difficult and obscure position because of your stance on faith, remember to look for the task God has assigned to you. How do we know what this task is? We begin by looking at what we are gifted to do and where our talents are. God would not have given us gifts if He did not plan for us to use them for His glory.

From Genesis to Revelation, when looking at faith, one thing is sure: God will test your faith. Relying on anything means that it must first be tested before it can be trusted.

Scripture reveals an interesting pattern in the development of faith and a similar development can be seen throughout history in the lives of people we see as leaders. Their lives show a short-term, steep curve in their faith development. This is seen in Jonah's life – from the storm at sea, to three days in the belly of a fish, to sitting in the sun and heat and wanting to die.

Other examples are Jesus' passion and resurrection; Peter's denial and restoration; Daniel in the lion's den; Daniel's friends in the fiery furnace; Esther appearing before the king on behalf of her people; Moses speaking to Pharaoh on behalf of Israel; Paul speaking to King Agrippa; Elijah at Mount Carmel; and Abraham's trials. All these people went through short-term dramatic events when their lives were severely tested and spiritually enhanced. It's interesting that during their most testing times, God was closer to them than ever before. They even had the privilege to dialogue with God. It's a time during which a deep relationship with God is forged and have a profound effect on their trust in God. When all safety nets, their Plan B and their reliance on self are brought to nothing. If it were not for these traumatic events, they would have gone their own way and disobeyed God. This short-term event emptied their hearts from all selfishness and arrogance.

Jonah's suffering was all a result of his choice to disobey God – instead of trusting God, he trusted his own plans and the event was designed by God to adjust his heart and thinking and to align them with God's plans. This short-term development changes the life of the believer. Because of the intensity of the event, the person undergoes a total transformation. From relying on self and their own wisdom in the natural realm, to walking by the Spirit, which is the realm of true faith that we're called to walk in, and it doesn't come without a true sacrifice; it strips you of all falsehood, bravado and it ends the rule of the flesh.

There is a crucial matter that emerges from every situation in Scripture where a short-term stay occurred. God is serious about the work He started and His salvation work is all about His eternal Kingdom. For it to move forward, He wants to ensure that the people who carry it can be trusted. His honour is on display and if a person cannot bear the weight and the responsibility entrusted to them, they should either be bypassed for leadership or be trained further to enable them to carry the burden. This is why those who walk by faith are guaranteed to see their faith tested. God's work is weighty and testing ensures that the person He chooses to work in His Kingdom matches His expectation. No person can go untested, not even Jesus.

Chapter 24

Watch your step

W hen a parcel is ordered to be delivered or when you a guest's imminent arrival is expected, any delays can be frustrating, especially if no word is received to explain the delay. In times of delays, a believer can lose focus and it is at this stage that mistakes are made.

Imagine if Joseph, a ruler in the making who was waiting for his destiny, had committed adultery with Potiphar's wife. Everything Abraham, Isaac and Jacob had fought for would have been lost in a few minutes. The nation of Israel would have looked very different if Joseph had conceived a son with the wife of the captain of Pharoah's guard. Joseph would have been very frustrated when his destiny was to be a ruler, based on his early childhood dreams.

Consider David's predicament when Saul was hunting him like a wild animal. David was deep in the cave when Saul came to relieve himself in the same cave (1 Samuel 24:1-6). Imagine if David had decided to kill Saul; what would have been the consequences for the one anointed to be Israel's next king? It's particularly noteworthy that David heard God's voice over his men's who said to him: "This is the day the Lord spoke of when he said to you, 'I will give your enemy into your hands for you to deal with as you wish.'" This was no small historical event; to hear God's voice and obey it when a life-threatening problem can be dealt with and people around you counsel you to proceed with it.

When Abraham was walking up Mount Moriah to go sacrifice his son, as instructed by God, imagine the thoughts, reasoning and plans going around in his head about killing his only son of promise. He carried God's instructions in secret and had to fight off any thoughts of doubt and anxiety. Imagine if Abraham had decided not to follow through or if he had uttered words he would regret later. His state of mind could have been very different as he lifted his knife to kill Isaac and he may not have heard God speak to him about the ram stuck in the thickets (Genesis 22:13). God could have brought Isaac back to life, but the main concern would have been Abraham's disobedience to God's command.

Soft voice of the Spirit

Today we have the soft voice of the Holy Spirit speaking to us and guiding us. Personally, I've not heard Him speak in the form of a loud thunderbolt. His voice is generally soft and brief. If we choose to walk in sin, our relationship with God would be damaged and when this happens, we will not hear His voice. This will lead to mistakes on our part and cause great suffering into the future. It's therefore important that we watch our step carefully when we are walking through the fields of delays.

In periods of delay, believers are vulnerable and weak. The enemy is crafty and he knows this and he shoots his fiery darts to try and persuade us to turn his way. It's therefore in our best interest to turn to God, to transfer the problem into God's hands completely to prevent us from making crucial errors or falling into the enemy's trap.

A person standing on the edge of a cliff is vulnerable and similarly, a person who has been walking through the fields of delays is also vulnerable. One wrong move and they could fall off the edge. As in the case of Jonah, it's often small and seemingly unimportant things that could cause a person to fall off the edge (Jonah 4:6-11). To Jonah, it was the small tree that provided his shade. When it was removed, he was angry and started sulking.

Be careful of the tail

The following is a warning of how the enemy will attempt to deceive and destroy the believer's faith. Every believer must develop a sense of an awareness of the enemy's tactics, the methods he employs and his end goal. Many believers live in ignorance of the enemy's ways and suffer in their faith for it. 2 Corinthians 2:11 says that one of the enemy's tactics is to get involved where strife and forgiveness occur among believers in a community. Using this scenario, he can defeat the believers and gain an advantage over them.

There are several parts to a prolonged waiting period when walking by faith. As mentioned earlier, patience is key, but so too is being careful what you say and do while you wait. When we're tired and frustrated, we more easily let our guard down and allow the enemy to gain a foothold in our lives. As believers, we need to be careful and not careless.

We need to be on the lookout for what is described in Revelation 12:3-4 as the ancient serpent. He is depicted as a red dragon who was thrown out of heaven and as he left, he swept a third of the angels out of heaven with his tail. It was as if the process to rid heaven of the evil one was almost over when the dragon played a final trick on his way out. When most beings believed he had left heaven, with his long tail trailing behind him, he collected a multitude of angels to join his cause.

When we've worked hard and waited patiently, it's important not to let our guard down at that stage. The enemy hates those who walk by faith because he's powerless against them. By inviting God in to help them, they step out of the way and the enemy must contend with God – a fight he will never win. But be careful not to neglect his tail and the damage it can cause. Never let your guard down when walking by faith; wait patiently and be observant and alert. Paul urges us to fight in the spiritual realm. He says we are to do everything we can to stand our ground, "and after you have done everything, to stand" (Ephesians 6:13 NIV). He is urging believers not to become complacent and careless.

On a personal note, I've learnt that when the pressure becomes too much to bear, you're at risk of making mistakes. It is then that an interesting phenomenon becomes apparent. Either you totally surrender to God and allow Him to take over or you allow the tail of the dragon to sweep you away. I can personally testify to this. At the point when I felt totally overwhelmed, I sat on the floor and just prayed to my Lord for help. It felt as if I had exhausted all options and that I was left with no answer or solution. That was when I experienced and witnessed the immediate hand of God in my situation. I believe God was waiting for that specific moment of total surrender that would allow Him to act. Perhaps I had been preventing Him from acting on my behalf because I had been trying so hard to get things done. The choice I faced wat to either surrender to God or get upset, which would inevitably lead to me saying or doing something unhelpful.

My advice is to pull up the handbrake, sit down and pray. Surrender your all before God so that He can act on your behalf. Not surrendering means that you are resisting God and you will be swept away by the enemy's tail through your words or actions. The enemy knows your weaknesses; he knows how to get under your skin. He will personalise his strategies to get your attention. Once he does, he will be relentless in his pursuit of your destruction.

Beaten to a pulp

When I was a child, I used to watch my mother make mince in the kitchen. She took large pieces of meat, cut them into cubes and then fed them into the mincing machine. What came out the other side was mince, which didn't resemble the meat cubes anymore and had changed completely. The mince was red meat, but in a finely cut mushy form. The believer who embarks on a faith walk will feel as if they're going through a similar process, undergoing chopping and cutting, pressure and transforming of their nature.

The believer's walk of faith will grow in intensity with time as their flesh ends its rule. This is described as crucifixion of the flesh, when the person's will and their dependency on it is put to death. Every believer has followed their own will, desires and ways. Unless this force is not put to death, it will always resurrect itself and step in to rule over the person's life.

The enemy with its dragon tail is bent on destroying our hope and our trust in God. Even when we feel beaten down, the enemy's tail will come to steal from us, which will make the situation even more unbearable and can feel as if the enemy has had the final say. We need to avoid becoming complacent or careless because e never stops pursuing the believer. But no matter how weak we feel, one thing is true, God is in all, overall and above all.

Isaiah 40:31 says those who trust in God get a special empowerment and that even though they might feel tired and defeated, He will strengthen them.

> … those who hope in the Lord will renew their strength.
> They will soar on wings like eagles; they will run and not
> grow weary, they will walk and not be faint. Isaiah
> 40:31 (NIV)

Verse 29 says He will give strength to the weary – this is not a strength from within themselves nor is it human resilience to keep fighting and prevail until a victory is won. Isaiah 40 speaks of a people who are already beaten down and don't see a way out of their struggle; they have no more hope. They get up and are beaten down again, causing their will to be broken and their escape plans brought to naught. This process also symbolises the beatings that a believer endures in surrendering their will and plans and abandoning their self-reliance.

On the cross, Jesus surrendered all He was and all He could have done. His hope was in His Father. This is a journey that the spiritual believer must also experience. We tend to rely on our strong will, resilience to succeed and our creative problem-solving minds. Only in death can these powerful obstacles to true faith be set aside – not a physical death, but the death to self, death to a reliance on anything else but God. Jesus made this clear in Matthew 16:23-26. He said that anyone who wants to follow Him must first deny themselves then take up their cross and follow Him. Before you can take up the cross, which is the symbol of death to the old nature, there must be a willingness to do so as expressed in the words, "they must deny themselves" (Matthew 16:24). No one can do this for someone else.

To deny yourself is reflected in Proverbs 3:5,6, which says that trusting in the Lord leaves no space for self-reliance or indeed reliance on any human wisdom. The inverse is also true. Verse 23 says that if you do trust in the Lord with all your heart, your foot will not stumble. Jesus later said human concerns can be a stumbling block to doing the things of God (Matthew 16:23). To follow Jesus, to walk in complete trust as He did with His Father, it took the cross as a symbol of death, to demonstrate to us what is needed to end reliance on ourselves.

The fact is that when Jesus was at His weakest physically, when His enemies seemed to have triumphed over Him, He was at His strongest. He was at His Father's mercy. It's worth reminding ourselves that His Father was God over all – over death and life, over every power and dominion. There is no one above Him. The weaker the believer is in the realm of self-reliance, the more powerful they are in their faith in God.

It is true that sometimes our beating is prolonged and seems overly harsh, but it is in direct relation to the time it takes to end our self-reliance. True faith is not meant to rely on the flesh, on ourselves. True faith is designed to bring a person's boasting to an end before it can be honoured by God. In 2 Corinthians 12:9,10, Paul states that God's power is perfected in our lives during times of weakness when we experience testing.

But he said to me, "My grace is sufficient for you, for my power is made perfect in weakness." Therefore I will boast all the more gladly about my weaknesses, so that Christ's power may rest on me. That is why, for Christ's sake, I delight in weaknesses, in insults, in hardships, in persecutions, in difficulties. For when I am weak, then I am strong. 2 Corinthians 12:9,10 (NIV)

Chapter 25

Making mental notes

I t's not uncommon that people don't remember a sermon they've just heard because in many instances, people have developed lazy minds and have lost the ability to take mental notes. One way to combat a lazy mind is to get them to make written notes in a notebook. This is a way to keep their minds engaged during a sermon and it ensures that the message goes with them during the week as they recap what was said using their notes.

A helpful practice for people walking by faith is to know what to do when the delays begin to feel like the denials. This is almost never true, but it is how our minds interpret things. When we don't see or experience God's intentional hand in our request, we put words into His mouth and we allow doubt to become the leading direction we go in.

When we're faced with delays, a key step is not to become idle and passive. This is a minefield and the enemy will almost always prevail against us here. A passive mind is like an engine running out of fuel; it's only a question of time and the momentum is lost. A person who remains active in their daily work, their prayer-time, Bible reading and worship are not as easily swayed by a delay.

A helpful way to combat doubt when we experience a delay is to refer to a previous testing time we went through and remind ourselves what it felt like, what we did and how the Lord came to our rescue. By doing this we remind ourselves of the need for delays and how to handle them. This is important because every time we experience a delay, the enemy seems able to convince us that this is the first time this has happened.

How do we beat this monster of delays? Well, we need irrefutable evidence, which we get from the delay we are facing. We need to push through the delay to receive God's provision, and while we're pushing through, we make mental and written notes. We intentionally write down what we're experiencing during the delay; we note how we're bombarded by thoughts of doubt and uncertainty; and we note how we feel.

How will this help us? This exercise prepares us for the next faith challenge and our written and mental notes form irrefutable evidence of God's goodness and faithfulness. Those written reminders serve as a bridge over a wide chasm, carrying us from the moment we make our need known to God, through the time of uncertainty when it feels as if we're dangling in mid-air, to when we received our answer on the other side. When we put our minds to work, when we take notes, we prevent negativity from taking hold and we strengthen our resolve to trust God no matter what. What we've experienced in the past could well be the key to a victorious future – if we can remember what we have learnt in the past.

How I settle my mind

During a period of a specific faith journey, I felt as if I was in an intense battle. Bad news, negative friends, unexpected events all contributed to what looked like dark clouds approaching me. I felt both helpless, angry and confused at the same time. I began questioning my convictions because no matter how hard I tried to focus my mind on a particular desired outcome, the reality around me was unfriendly. I learnt quickly not to look to people or circumstances to find certainty. It seemed that today's victory was quickly undone by tomorrow disaster and nothing seemed to be certain.

I decided to meditate on the two verses in Philippians 4:6,7 where Paul gives us the desired steps to settle our minds. Living in a world full of false anchors, every believer needs an anchor in a storm because we will be steered into a storm to test and purify our faith (1 Peter 1:7).

Philippians 4:6,7 says that when we present our requests before God, there will be a time of delay when our minds will be faced with either accepting what the eyes can see or what God has said. Paul describes this as the peace of God that transcends all understanding will guard your hearts and minds in Christ Jesus. It means that what God says will oppose reality or reality will oppose God's Word, which delivers something the mind cannot agree to. Nothing this world offers is guaranteed and no believer should place their hope in it.

When we make our request known to God and we place our trust in Him, we receive the peace of God, and this is what we need to replace what the world cannot give. God is unchangeable and when we walk in His Word, we place our hope and trust in something unchangeable. His peace operates on a level higher than our thinking and reasoning.

Stand strong in the battle

Faith battles are always tough because faith is how we inherit eternal life and how we walk victoriously in a world hostile to God and those who follow Him (Romans 1:17 and Hebrews 11:6). No reward worth eternal value will be given away cheaply.

Sometimes it feels as if we're being crushed from all sides with no way to escape and we need to remember that the "big squeeze" is there to purge us from what opposes God's Word and His will.

Before a dirty glass of water can be filled with pure water, its contents must be poured out, the glass cleaned and only then can pure water be poured into the glass. It's necessary for us to be emptied first and washed before we can be developed; a dirty glass cannot clean itself.

In the trenches of faith, we become what we cannot achieve by ourselves and we undergo a change that we cannot achieve under normal circumstances. Worldly success gained through worldly means is like dust that gathers on a table; it's quickly wiped away. But faith victories, which embody eternal values and rewards within the believer's heart, can never be lost or wiped out.

Strength through faith comes when we feel as if we are totally spent, exhausted and overwhelmed. Realisation that we've been relying on our own strength comes to us when we reach the end of our human strength and wisdom, when we understand that we cannot accomplish anything worthy in God's eyes (John 15:5).

Tired and desperate we give in to God's Spirit and we begin to realise that we are stronger than before. We become dependent on God's eternal Spirit because we're not relying on our own limited abilities. It's when we've been emptied of ourselves that we begin to develop a heavenly joy. How can we be joyful when we're beaten down? Because we realise that we don't have to make it work and we feel stronger than ever because we feel Jesus' hand holding ours. We have given Him our problem and we can rely on His power for all we need. This is how we can be joyful.

Transformation in the trenches

When we're in the trenches fighting faith battles, we undergo significant transformation and we begin to live supernatural lives in a natural world. Our thinking, words and actions become those of Jesus and they transcend the understanding of our broken world. We begin to live eternally while we're in a finite world with all its problems and limitations. There's nothing sweeter; it's the reward of faith, which comes after you've stood your ground and have your request granted by God. No manmade success, achievement or worldly acknowledgement can compare to the reward of faith.

The rest everyone desires

When a house has been constructed with a sound foundation and strong structure, it will remain standing for many years, because of the work that was done in the initial construction phase. The home owner can rest assured that the building will prevail against the harshest weather – and they can live in it with a sense of peace and security.

True rest is something people cannot secure by themselves; the knowledge that their present and future is secure is worth all the money in the world and people go to great lengths to achieve that rest. But rest in humanity's terms is impossible in a world where nothing is secure. Jesus invited the people to come to Him, because He said they will find rest where He is (Matthew 11:28,29). This is a conditional rest, where gentleness, humility and a personal decision are required. We don't obtain rest until we've laid down what we're busy with.

During the faith project I earlier referred to, there were times when I felt as if I was drowning. At night when I lay awake, I felt as if I was being sucked under in white water rapids and I was fighting to come up for air. I was working through dozens of "what if" scenarios and after many hours, I still had no plan how to solve the assault on our financial future. The situation was out of my hands all I could do was to wait. I had sent messages and emails, made many calls, seen people and placed advertisements – nothing helped. Throughout this time, I knew that God was for me and by then I had prayed for days on end with no clear solution.

One night I had a brief vision of a person suspended about two metres above the ground in a beam of light. The person was lying on their back fully trusting the beam of light that held them up. I woke up and decided I was going to do exactly what Abraham had done, what Jesus did on the cross, and what so many of God's faith heroes in history had done – they put their total trust in God. They rested from their work, from their anxious concerns and they put their hope in the creator of the universe, their Father in heaven.

Let me assure you, this was not an easy task. Every single day was a fight to leave my burden at God's feet. It sometimes felt like split-second decision-making not to take back the weight of my problem. The moment my mind drifted, when I was not attentive, it felt as if a flood of worry filled the room and all the anxiety came rushing back. I had to learn to be diligent not to venture into the area of thoughts where my problems were located, especially at night. In time I became a policeman of my thought life. I would guard against drifting and negative thoughts and upsetting news. I told myself that the problem is not mine anymore.

The diligent policing of my thoughts allowed me to form a pattern of finding peace in the midst of a harsh reality. Everything that looked very worrying, I passed onto my Father in heaven and I thanked him every day for carrying my load and I started a daily routine of handing my cares over to Him. When I did it, peace would come over me. My breathing slowed down, my diet returned to normal, and I was able to watch my temper. I felt more connected to God than ever before. It seemed as if I had entered a new level in my spiritual walk that I hadn't experienced before and my relationship with the Spirit of God had deepened. With time I could hear His voice clearer and when I picked up my Bible to read and study, the depth of revelation was by far greater than before.

One morning I read Hebrews 4 that speaks of the rest of God. It referenced Israel's historical Old Testament journey from Egyptian slavery, their wandering in the Wilderness and then finally inhabiting the Promised Land. I had read these accounts many times and could sense their anxiety when they, a small nation of shepherds, had to face great powerful nations. What struck me though, was when God said He refused entry into the Promised Land to those who did not have faith in Him. Ultimately the unbelieving Israelites heard God's promise, they saw His deliverance, they tasted His provision for them as a nation every day for more than forty years, and still they did not trust God to inhabit the Promised Land, the place where God would reside among His people and where their enemies would be subdued. 2 Samuel 7:1,2 speaks of David entering God's rest, and as soon as David rested, he began planning the temple of the Lord. His focus changed and he had time to plan the things that the nation needed.

Jesus gave an open invitation to anyone who's feeling overwhelmed in Matthew 11:28,29. He said we are to hand our burdens to Him, place our trust in Him and take up His yoke. Then we will receive the rest so many people yearn for; a rest that settles all arguments and reasonings that flood our minds. It's a rest and an assurance that we're in a safe place. This rest comes from a documented example of Israel's history. It's not blind faith nor subjective hope. This rest stems from God's Word Who walked earth and Who invites me to place my burden in His hands and take up His yoke, which is to obey His Father's commands. This in turn unlocks great favour from God (1 John 5:3). Jesus' burden was to do His Father's will and in being obedient, He secured eternal life for everyone who would believe in Him. His burden has now become my burden. Both Jesus and the Apostle Paul urged us not to carry our own burdens, for this is contrary to the will of God (Matthew 6:25-33 and Philippians 4:6).

My newfound rest is challenged daily by the enemy who uses people to bring me negative reports and events that are designed to discourage my faith. It has taken real effort to maintain my trust in the face of so much opposition in the spirit realm, but I came to find it easier to enter my 'safe place' when anxious thoughts resurfaced. I grew in my ability to discern moments when I needed to specifically guard my thoughts and utterances. This became a very private battle because the more I put it out there, the more I felt people would in ignorance want to give unhelpful advice or make negative comments.

Have tasted the rest I now have, I wouldn't exchange it for anything in this world. It's an assurance only found in Jesus; no amount of scientific analysis, statistical formulation or hard work can accumulate the trust I have in my Father's Word. If He was faithful to those in Israel who put their trust in Him, then so I can find the rest in my solid foundation, Jesus Christ, in the midst of the financial storm.

Chapter 26

Developing a secure foothold

C an the believer reach a point where their faith is beyond challenging? Can a person's faith be described as immovable? Can a believer become truly convinced of an outcome in their faith?

The Word of God describes faith as a spiritual gift that's administered to us by the Spirit of God (1 Corinthians 12:9). This means faith is not human in origin, it originates from God and it's a gift, like a seed sown into the heart of the believer. If it is nurtured and watered, it will produce after its own nature. Faith or trust in God is measurable in that God rewards us to the extent that we trust Him (Hebrews 11:6).

With time and through trials, a believer's faith becomes solid. It's very similar to the process cement goes through when used in construction. Initially faith is rather fluid and can be altered, but when it is boxed, its shape is established. After it is mixed with water, a chemical process takes place and the cement hardens. In Scripture we see how a believer's faith starts off weak, but after seasons of testing and trials, their faith becomes solid. No matter the threats, pain or discomfort the believer may suffer, their faith in God will remain.

In any construction process, a foundation must be established before the building takes place. It's for this reason that Scripture states that Jesus is our sure foundation (Matthew 7:24,25). Whatever is built in Christ is secure and faith is how we build on Jesus our foundation. According to the proper Bible interpretation, faith is not a stand-alone principle that the believer lives by. It starts with a single seed, call it a small decision, which develops into a large fruit-bearing tree. Paul describes faith in the context of a relationship when he mentions the three important spiritual principles of hope, faith and love (1 Corinthians 13:4-13). This relationship is the seedbed for a solid foundation. Once this base has strengthened and solidified like cement, it becomes an unbreakable eternal foundation. Faith in the life of the believer is the door to salvation. Faith also forms the spiritual foundation on which Jesus builds every spiritual principle into the life of the believer. Hebrews 12:2 says Jesus is the author and the one who matures our faith; once He is our foundation, our faith (trust in God) becomes unshakeable.

Faith needs time

Faith alone is not what makes us strong. As cement needs steel reinforcing to strengthen it, so faith needs time and trials to reach maturity. I call these trails faith testers and they come our way to purify our faith. They also come with the full approval of God. Trials test our faith and in many cases, the impurities in us are exposed. Often these are our emotions, our dependence on our own strength and our lack of trust in God. These faith testers are not sent to destroy us, but to develop us. Many believers misunderstand faith testers because they become unhappy when experiencing setbacks. Believe me, no testing is pleasant and no severe trial is welcomed. However, once we've endured a storm, we celebrate the fact that our faith capacity has been enlarged and it enables us to become triumphant in life. It enables us to weather increasingly testing storms. Our new faith capacity is the faith of Jesus Himself, which has developed in us to enable us to be like Him (John 16:33).

Temptation and testing

Scripture gives us two kinds of events we will experience. One is temptation and the other is testing. While the former is there to destroy us, the latter is there to develop us. God allows both in our lives as a means of maturing us. Our faith develops from infancy to maturity, where we can withstand any attack from the enemy. Our faith will and must be challenged; as scientific tests are performed on products to certify their quality and strength, so our faith can only be measured when it gets tested as we can see in Hebrews 11, which tells how the heroes of the faith remained steadfast in trusting God even in the face of death.

During the process of developing our faith, there are two crucial aspects we must understand and treat separately. Should these two be confused, we could end up misapplying our faith and damaging the relationship we have with God. The two aspects are the faith project and the relationship we have with God. They're part of the process of faith, but one is a primary and the other a secondary aspect. The relationship we have with God is birthed within us by the Spirit of God when He enables us to cry Abba Father (Romans 8:15-17) at the point of justification by grace through faith. This relationship is the primary aspect in the believer's faith walk and its strength is determined by the maturity of the relationship over time.

It's not the tenacity of the believer who chooses to keep trusting God, it is God's faithfulness (Numbers 23:19) that solidifies the evidence handed to the believer. The faith project is a later secondary step that relies exclusively on the primary aspect of faith – the relationship with God.

God is the One who matures our faith and the stronger our relationship with God, the greater the trust and ore certainty we have that God will answer our prayers. Within the time of testing and maturing, the believer learns how to manage their thoughts and emotions. The greatest testing time is between the moment the believer puts their faith in God and the moment the answer or outcome of the faith project is received. It's in this time that the believer's emotions and mind play key roles in the development of the relationship.

Many believers have succeeded in walking through a time of testing and received the answer to their prayers. They've held onto God for what they needed and through this process have grown in their faith. However, when we read Hebrews carefully, we see that chapter eleven mentions a faith that we still need to develop. This is a faith that doesn't require a completion of the project. It's a trust in God that He will deliver, even after death. True faith in God spans this life and the life to come. The trust in the relationship is the barometer of the believer's ability to wait on God, even unto death.

We can see this in the relationship between a believer and God when the person is about to breath their last. Over a lifetime, the believer has had three facets that played a key role in the maturing of their faith – their reliance on the Word of God, factual evidence of God's faithfulness and their personal experience when trusting God. Together these three have been instrumental in cementing the believer's faith in God. When they close their eyes for the last time, there isn't a shred of doubt in their being about where they'll re-open their eyes. Their Father's bosom awaits them and no power, no person and no deception can shake their trust in God.

It's about keeping on

Faith is like a muscle in a bodybuilder's arm; the more they work it the stronger it becomes. The muscle doesn't develop when the athlete puts the weight down, but only when the muscle is working with a weight – it's resistance that strengthens the muscle.

In the same way, the believer who walks by faith is like an athlete who exercises their faith and who experiences resistance by an unseen enemy. Each time the believer exercises their faith and feels the resistance to trust God, their faith conviction gets stronger. Resistance can take the form of various circumstances such as opposition, sickness, oppression, lack of resources, intimidation, contextual frustrations and struggles. God allows these to strengthen the believer. In the spirit, faith is met with opposition every time it is exercised, and when faith it is, the enemy sets out to oppose the believer to wear them down to the point that they give up.

God wants the believer to not give up and He invites them to exercise their faith and trust that He'll come to their rescue. Opposition pursues the believer who walks by faith; once they exercise their faith, they become stronger in their faith conviction and God rewards them (Hebrews 11:6).

The believer who has identified the enemy's scheme of opposition and intimidation when exercising their faith, is a believer whose faith is as strong as cement. As the law of gravity spares no person, equally the enemy spares no believer's faith activities and he will oppose every person who puts their trust in God. With time and use, the believer's trust in the Word of God becomes unchallengeable.

Starting small and continuing to work against opposition will equip the believer to live a life of faith. Growth comes when the believer exercises their faith daily and not just in times of distress and need. God gave the gift of faith to every believer to enable them to develop holistically to maturity and holiness. When faith, through frequent use, replaces personal reliance, it becomes a powerful force in the life of a believer.

God has determined a life of faith for the believer because it comes as package deal with predetermined good works that please God (Ephesians 2:10). Continuing to walk by faith will keep inviting opposition, but it will also enable the believer to keep pleasing God in all they do. Keeping on keeping on will result in a great eternal reward saved up for the believer.

Chapter 27

The heavenwards faith spiral

But one thing I do: forgetting what is behind and straining towards what is ahead, I press on towards the goal to win the prize for which God has called me heavenwards in Christ Jesus. Philippians 3:13b;14 (NIV)

Here Paul is describing a process, not an event. He uses the metaphor of an athlete who trains and prepares themself for a great event – to successfully reach the finish line. While the athlete is in the race, they're undergoing a transformation towards Christian maturity. The heavenwards call Paul refers to is a progressive development to a higher level – a deeper relationship with God. He says what's needed are spiritual disciplines and strict training. This process resembles an upward spiral that starts small, but with time it develops into a wide spiral which completely transforms the believer.

Several years ago, I read a book by Derek Prince on spiritual warfare and the demands this ministry put on him and his family.

His frequent exorcisms caused him to walk around with a target on his back. Setting people free from the enemy's clutches doesn't make the enemy happy and he'll come after you again and again to intimidate or hurt you and your family. It's tough to maintain a ministry or a lifestyle whereby you plunder hell and promote the Kingdom of God. What I gleaned from Derek Prince was that living by faith is the very thing God desires and the enemy hates.

The warfare that takes place in the spirit world when a person is walking by faith, is similar to conducting exorcisms. Faith upsets the flesh; it opposes the enemy's schemes and most importantly, it glorifies God. Walking by faith means death to the flesh and living by the Spirit of God. A true faith walk is not for the faint hearted.

Jesus is a King who came to do war against an eternal enemy. He said He didn't come to bring peace, but a holy sword (Matthew 10:34-36). A life of faith is truly a radical life, and it's a life lived on this earth using supernatural means. These two realms are always in conflict with each other. To walk by faith, the believer must develop a life lived in the spirit, which will make them indifferent to the principles of this world (Galatians 4:3). Inevitably, this will place a heavy toll on the believer, just as Derek Prince testified.

A life of faith can resemble the story of Daniel in the lion's den. Daniel was closely watched by his enemies who wanted to destroy him and throw him to the hungry lions. Believers need to be alert and on the lookout for efforts to destroy your faith in God. When a Christian decides to trust God fully and walk by faith, they will need to be on their guard – walking by faith is like living in a warzone.

Can believers stand up to the enemy?

Did God then predestine the believer to face an invincible enemy? Will the believer, who truly walks by faith, be able to stand up to the enemy? Believer who walk by faith in God will be targeted by the enemy and they must develop a heavenwards, or upward faith spiral, that keeps developing. The believer must steadfastly remain in God's Word – reading, studying, meditating and pausing at specific passages until they receive revelation from the Spirit about the specific passage.

God's Word brings light (Psalm 119:130) that cannot be hidden. It attracts the enemy who wants to choke the Word, discredit it and stop every bit of growth it produces. It's crucial that a believer who's walking by faith spends time edifying themselves and growing in spiritual authority. Soon the believer will need to visit the Word more often to draw on the revelation they glean from it and spend more time in prayer. By now the believer has begun developing an upward faith spiral. The more they study and pray, the more their spirit is edified and emboldened and the more they can withstand the enemy's attacks (Ephesians 6:11). As their Word content increases, so does their faith and so do the enemy's attacks – in quantity and quality. Believers develop to a point where they can identify the enemy's plans, patterns and strategies through their knowledge and understanding of God's Word and their growth will enable them to grow in spiritual authority and pre-empt the enemy's attack.

Waging constant war

The believer must not be presumptuous and think that an evil strongman will easily give up his territorial stronghold and the souls in it. Walking by faith requires that the believer wages war for every forward step. Growth in spiritual authority is only possible after a victory in the spirit realm. Once the enemy has lost territory, he will return to regain it – even if he takes a long time to do so.

A deeper involvement in the spiritual world will cause the believer to hunger for more of God's Word and the spiritual wisdom and authority it brings. Greater depth in God's Word releases greater revelation, which opens the believer's eyes even more to the spiritual world. An important fact is that greater revelation causes the believer to acknowledge their need for God more than ever. The upward faith spiral will demonstrate to the believer that they cannot accomplish anything God-worthy in their own strength and wisdom. The world of the flesh, the natural world, has no authority in the spirit world, which has authority over the natural world. This is the reason the believer must develop an upward faith spiral to walk in the spirit more than in the flesh.

Not by faith alone

The upward faith spiral demonstrates an important spiritual principle. A believer cannot grow spiritually by only focusing on faith and they cannot fight off the enemy by employing faith alone. Faith is often incorrectly presented as a stand-alone spiritual force, as sometimes perceived by believers who see the Spirit of God as a force and not a person of the Trinity. The Spirit is the giver of faith and He also releases power to the believer when petitioned to do so in prayer, but He's not a power.

When faith is seen or practiced as a single step and not a discipline that forms part of a process, spiritual maturity cannot be achieved by the believer. By applying faith as a single principle to spiritual maturity, all the believer will develop is a power-hungry arrogance. Remember that the goal of faith is first to glorify God and second to play a part in the believer's journey to spiritual maturity (Philippians 3:12-14).

I believe faith has a shelf-life so that when spiritual maturity has been reached in heaven, faith is no longer needed (1 Corinthians 13:13). For the believer to receive the reward of spiritual maturity, which the heavenwards call of God (Philippians 3:14), they must undergo several spiritual developmental steps. Here, the understanding and application of spiritual principles or disciplines in God's Word are crucial. The heavenwards call of God is understood to resemble something resembling the upward spiritual faith spiral. It's God's desire that the believer matures, just as any parent wants to see their infant grow and develop into maturity.

The believer must grasp several important spiritual principles. The first is faith, which is expressing our trust in God and it begins with a knowledge and understanding of God's Word (Romans 10:17).

As the believer's knowledge and understanding of God's Word increases, so does their trust in God and their reliance on themselves, which is an expression of humility. When humility increases, the Spirit of God has more freedom to begin the process of sanctification, which in turn leads the believer to a life of progressive obedience and increasing holiness. The realm of the spirit now becomes the believer's dominant realm as the flesh and its sinful desires are subdued by the Spirit.

The spiritual journey enables further developmental steps in the life of the believer, which must take place by introducing additional spiritual principles. Jesus demonstrated many different principles during His life on earth and finally on the cross that every believer must master. Jesus had to undergo spiritual development to demonstrate what's needed by every believer (Hebrews 5:8). Throughout His life, Jesus exemplified the spiritual principles of true humility and spiritual authority, He displayed the fruits of the Spirit, and He walked in obedience to His Father's will with a true servant's heart. Jesus placed His life into His Father's hands even though He had all authority to end His suffering (Matthew 26:53). Jesus made it clear that authority is expressed in humble servant-hood (John 13:12-17).

Faith taken out of context and not yoked to a servant-hearted humility, obedience and desire to walk in God's will has the poten-tial to breed selfish ambition and fleshly boasting. If we express faith as trust in God, we need to ask ourselves to what extent can God trust us with the authority He has invested in us. Paul, having been given great spiritual authority on earth, stated that his only aim was to know Jesus and to share in His sufferings (Philippians 3:10-12). As Jesus emptied Himself (Philippians 2:7), His upward faith spiral brought Him to the right hand of God the Father on the throne.

While the spiral works its way upwards, the believer's increased Word knowledge will give rise to interesting spiritual development as it allows the Holy Spirit greater scope to work. The believer will experience an increase in understanding, discernment, wisdom and discretion which will lead to a change as their life in the spirit begins to dictate their conduct and decision-making. They will yield more to the promptings of the Spirit than that of the flesh.

Paul said to that the Word of God washes the believer. At the point of salvation, a person experiences justification. The next step is sanctification, which is expressed as a purification of the believer – a step no person in their own strength and wisdom can accomplish. The or progression initiated by faith brings this present continuous phase of regeneration into the life of the believer; their spiritual understanding deepens and they're also purified as the Word washes them. Faith, as part of this upward spiral, is one step in a multiplex-event taking place in the life of a believer.

Here I have described the faith spiral in the life of a believer, which starts with faith and as the believer is progressively purified by the other spiritual principles that faith gives rise to. The process is designed to strip away worldliness and sinful desires as the believer is transformed to be more like Christ daily and a realisation sets in about how dependent they are on God's Word for everything they do and say.

Chapter 28

The effects of faith

H ere I'm including a few examples of the effect faith has in the life of the believer, which transforms the believer in many ways.

True faith will lead to obedience (Romans 1:5), which in turn will attract the blessings of God (Isaiah 1:19-20). One of these blessings is to enter God's rest (Hebrews 4:10).

The history of Israel in Scripture is clear – obedience leads the believer to God's rest. Through obedience the believer lays down their efforts and allows God to work in and through them. Faithless efforts only create problems and entanglements for the believer. But when they follow God's wisdom, which is the way that leads to life, they don't fall into the pitfalls of disobedience by following their own minds and the enemy's voice.

The essence of faith is empowering the believer to accomplish what they cannot do in their own power, efforts and wisdom. The effect of true faith emulates a son who lovingly honours his father with the respect and dignity that a father deserves.

The effects of choosing a way apart from faith is to abandon God and His Word and it leads to a path that the person regards as sound wisdom. Israel's history is a picture of a people who were called by God, who received God's commands and who had God walking with them and among them, yet they chose to disobey Him. Their downfall was evident. Many fell in the Wilderness and those who entered the Promised Land could not hold onto their promised inheritance.

Passages such as Deuteronomy 28 and Isaiah 1:19-20 say God's blessings will come to those who obey Him and they state the result of not obeying God. In Romans 1:17, Paul doesn't give the believer any alternative other than to walk by faith. Its impact on the life of a believer is crucially important – they're born again, then sanctified, then glorified. Over time, the effects of faith and the resulting obedience transform a sinner into a believer and into a mature person who walks with God in the Spirit – and the benefits of their faith become increasingly evident.

Faith depends on the Word of God being effective in the believer's life. The greater the Word content in our life, the more the Spirit of God has to work with to direct our steps. As the Word of God enters our hearts, the effect is that faith is released in our hearts to first convince us that we cannot accomplish what we need to in our own strength and wisdom.

Divide between flesh and spirit

An unspoken effect of faith is that we lay down fleshly desires and pursuits because faith opens our spiritual eyes and we see the divide between the flesh and the spirit. Faith awakens the desire to please God in us. Pleasing God is to obey God, but be careful here. We can only obey God when we become convinced in our hearts that our old ways are wrong. When we read God's Word, faith is released in our hearts to strive for obedience. This obedience brings God's blessings and the result is joy in our hearts.

The effect of faith is a change in our activities. Walking according to God's Word will ensure that we're in God's will. We hear His voice clearly and it guides us to where He is. Trusting Him becomes a pillar in our lives, stopping us when He stops and going when He goes. Faith will alter our routines, our actions and our spiritual effectiveness. By trusting God we'll walk into the place He has prepared for us. This is a life lived where God's blessings come upon us and overtake us.

Faith lifts our eyes from the struggles, battles and daily distractions around us so we can see the distant horizon. Faith is a gift so that we can accomplish God's purposes for us – something we cannot yet see nor accomplish ourselves. Faith will alert us regarding the future and will keep us from following our own path, keeping us on God's path designed for us. Only on this path will we find water in the desert; rest in times of war; increase in a famine and profit in recession. Like Israel, we will enter God's rest.

This was the fulfilment of the Promised Land. For Israel it was a physical land they had to conquer and settle in. For us today, our Promised Land is where God wants us to be – a place where He walks with us and dwells in us. It's a life of trusting God for provisions we cannot see and protection against the enemy whose very desire is to destroy us. Our Promised Land begins on this earth; we walk into it when we wake up in the morning, work during the day and put our heads down to sleep at night. The believer's walk of faith on earth is a preparation for the life to come. The promised heavenly dwelling Jesus spoke about begins for every believer at the point they are saved. Jesus said eternal life is to know God, which means that while we walk on earth we already experience God's presence, protection and provision (John 17:3).

Faith opens our eyes

Faith strips us from boasting (Ephesians 2:8-9) because it opens our eyes to the difference in God-ordained work and people's fruitless endeavours. Walking by faith draws us away from the enticements this world offers and opens our eyes to Godly wisdom, enabling us to see how this world's temptations are hooks in our flesh that can hurt us and prevent us from receiving the freedom God desires for us. Faith brings us to the place where we surrender our desires, plans and ambitions to God and where we invite His will and His ways. When we do, we see that what's done in God's will has God's blessing, provision and approval, and eternal life with Him.

Chapter 29

Results of walking by faith

Here are a few scenarios to describe some of the results a believer can experience when walking by faith.

There's no greater reward than achieving a desired result after many difficult days, hours or years or hard work – something that athletes and businesspeople alike celebrate.

Faith is the only door to salvation and sanctification. Sanctification is the gradual washing by the Word of God of the believer's daily words, thoughts and actions. At the point of salvation, faith acts as the ignition to rekindle the warmth between Gid and man. This is when a sinful person had their sins forgiven and is restored back into fellowship with God. Here, faith builds a deep eternal relationship of trust between man and God.

Faith initially secures the unbeliever's justification (Ephesians 2:8-9 and John 3:3-8). Being baptised by the Holy Spirit is different to being born again. Being empowered by the Holy Spirit releases all the gifts of the Spirit to the believer. Paul says those who believe receive the Holy Spirit and the seal of the Spirit (Ephesians 1:13-14).

Faith puts the ego and arrogance of the believer in the rubbish bin where it belongs. Without Jesus, no person can accomplish anything (John 15:4-5) and no flesh shall glorify itself in God's presence. Faith is letting go of a person's abilities, wisdom and strength, and allowing God to take control.

Faith is to hear God speak to us in His Word, after which we act on God's Word in trust. Faith allows us to hear God speak to us in a relationship and it helps us distinguish the enemy's voice by comparing it to the Word of God.

Faith glorifies God, because it accomplishes in this world what people cannot do, such as Jesus turning water into wine at the wedding in Cana; when He fed five thousand people; when He calmed the storm and many other instances.

Faith and sin have a few things in common. Both are lived out in the spirit realm, they affect the person's physical realm and both defy logic. When the serpent told Adam and Eve that they could be like God, this defied logic (Genesis 3:5). When Jesus called Peter out of the boat to walk on water, this also defied logic (Matthew 14:28).

Faith purifies the life of a believer. When the enemy pursues the believer to tempt and entrap them into sin, the believer can ask God to show them the origin and results of the sin. When the enemy's schemes are exposed by the Word of God, faith steps in by empowering the believer to see in the spirit what is truly taking place. This largely stops the believer from falling into the enemy's trap. By applying this process, the believer can walk free from sin.

Faith as a spiritual gift requires that the believer becomes more attentive to the voice and promptings of the Spirit of God and becomes more in tune with the Spirit. In doing so, the believer's ways will not follow the mainstream of this world. The believer will be able to take charge by the power of the Spirit wherever they are. Faith will bring friction between the believer and the world; it will attract the enemy's attention and to survive, the believer's walk in the Spirit will be an indispensable weapon.

Faith is the link that the believer has to petition God for the supernatural daily provisions they need. From a perspective and the context of the broken world we live in, it might sound absurd to think we need God's supernatural assistance. But, before Adam and Eve sinned, the earth was not cursed and what seems supernatural to us now, was normal for them before the fall.

Faith puts the deceptive pleasures and lures of worldly wealth in perspective compared with the promise of eternal riches. Faith ensures that the believer busies themself only with what God has planned for them, which means that greater things can be accomplished in a short space of time when God steps in, compared with a life spent toiling in human effort. When a believer walks by faith, they will, achieve less by human standards, but in God's eyes, they have achieved far more. Having God's blessings on your work (Hebrews 11:6) ensures greater pleasure to God and the believer's eternal inheritance will be greater.

Faith ensures that the believer is not roped into unnecessary battles that drain their resources, time and energy (1 Samuel 30:7-9).

Faith protects the believer from physical attacks that may harm or even destroy their bodies (Hebrews 1:14).

Faith can affect the decisions of crowds and save many lives. The expression of faith in many places in Scripture is an act of sheer obedience by a person after being commissioned by God. We can see how many lives are saved by Elijah when he acted against Jezebel's Ba'al prophets; when Jonah preached to Nineveh; when David fetched families taken captive by the Amalekites (1 Samuel 30:1-9) and when Jesus died on the cross.

Faith allows the believer to achieve their God-ordained purpose for their lives and in so doing, they expand the Kingdom of God. Like Abraham, when sent out of his native land to Canaan, he obeyed and became the father of the Jewish people. His faith in God not only gave him justification, it also gave birth to Isaac the patriarch.

True faith assures that every person lives in a level playing field. No human being is capable of elevating their spiritual status before God in their own strength. Because of Adam's sin, all of humanity needs God's grace and the gift of faith to be reconciled back to God. Faith is the first step a person takes to acknowledge they need God's forgiveness. Faith makes available God's plan of salvation to both king and beggar.

Faith secures the person's future, because their lives are in God's hands.

Faith provides the believer with an assurance of what they hope for (Hebrews 11:1). This assurance, which is based on God's faithfulness, brings a tremendous sense of peace to the believer.

Faith allows God to bless the person. Compare the blessings in Hebrews 11:6 with the passage of doubting Thomas in John 20:29.

Faith works in this life on earth and it allows the believer to live a natural life supernaturally. Faith empowers my daily life. If God did it for those who trusted Him, then He can also do it for me. As the person's faith develops with time, so do the supernatural results they will see on a daily basis. The person begins to live above worldly circumstances and in doing so, every challenge is taken to God in prayer. This way any anxiety is replaced with a surety that God will answer the person's prayer.

Faith turns an unbeliever into a believer and a believer into a grateful person. Thanksgiving is what God expects when He acts on our requests (Luke 17:15-17).

Faith acts as a shield against the enemy's attacks. The shield prevents the believer being struck and they walk free from injuries that could have been inflicted by the enemy. Faith allows the believer to trust God to warn them of impending danger and then avoid it.

Faith secures an eternal inheritance for the believer in the life to come. People may ask, 'Are we not to enjoy the present life? Are we placed on this earth just to endure it without any happiness or achievements? Do we merely endure this life and wait for the one to come? Jesus said that without Him we can do nothing (John 15:5). He didn't said we cannot achieve anything. What He did say is perfectly aligned with the core theme in Ecclesiastes 1:1-3, which says that everything under the sun is meaningless … The statement means that everything people achieve without God has no value. People can achieve great feats, yet they don't have value in God's eyes.

When a believer walks by faith, they walk in God's strength, not their own – and this has value in God's eyes (Hebrews 11:6). And the inverse of the theme in Ecclesiastes that everything is meaningless when done without God is that when things are done with God, there is eternal meaning.

Walking by faith gives meaning to what we do here on earth. Our earthly activities, when done by faith, secure eternal blessings and God's favour. When a believer becomes convicted of walking by faith, their activities begin to change to where they invest more in what carries eternal value. Their involvement in this world is reshaped; they begin to see earthly pleasures and possessions as meaningless, compared with what God values as eternal possessions.

When NASA counts down to a launch, they count down from ten to zero because every count has certain procedures and processes that need to take place before the final launch button can be pressed. In a similar way, when a person begins to walk by faith, certain processes and procedures develop in their lives. They do new things and stop doing old things and the entire process of faith leads to an expansion in their spiritual capacity. Faith is a gift of the Spirit and therefore walking by faith enables the believer to live in the spirit more than before.

The Spirit dictates to the natural realm and more attention is devoted to the Spirit, and less to the flesh. When a believer places their trust in God, they depend less on their own wisdom and strength and God's Word becomes their guide in everything they do. They see from Scripture how faithful God is and that He rewards those who put their trust in Him.

This trust aspect, centred in the relational walk with God and the growing Word content in their life, causes the believer to sin less. They are being washed by the water of the word, which is sanctification. Less sin means a stronger relationship between the believer and God.

Not only should the believer learn to trust God, they must also learn to earn God's trust by being faithful. The Spirit of God can replace the believer's futile thinking with instructions from God's Word. Scripture opens the believer's understanding and encourages them to follow the examples of many Biblical believers who put their trust in God. Faith leads to obedience in the believer's life. This helps them pursue the calling that God placed in their lives before birth.

By staying within the sphere of their calling and by avoiding pushing for a different office than God had ordained for them, they will be very fruitful in what they are doing.

By walking in the Spirit, better decisions are taken because the believer develops the spiritual gifts of discernment and discretion. Making better decisions will free them up to do more things that God calls them to. They will also discern what to say no to when applying their discretion and discernment. By doing less, they are actually doing more. By discerning what God wants them to do, they say no to flesh-driven deeds and attract God's blessings in all they do. Only doing what God has called them to declutters the believer's life and enables them to hear the voice of the Spirit clearer. When a believer can follow the lead of the Spirit, they're able to discharge the work God has called them to with great clarity and authority. As their spiritual capacity develops, the believer can launch their service to the Kingdom of God higher than before, because as they count down, all the required processes and procedures fall into place.

A new lifestyle

Walking by true faith can be described as follows: if a person relies on a walking aid to move around daily, then they have become used to the aid and cannot do without it. The use of the aid becomes a lifestyle and every day demands that they use it. They cannot see themselves living without it and other people get used to seeing them with the aid. Likewise, a person who embarks on a life of faith begins to rely on it and cannot exist without it.

Removing the veil

When Jesus said a person who walks by faith can move mountains, He was hinting at two obvious things. First, the challenge you're facing is beyond your power and ability to overcome or move out of the way. Without faith, the accomplishing gift from God, the mountain will not move, nor can you progress. Second, once a mountain is moved, you will not return to your old way of doing things. Once you've tasted God's gift and placed your trust in Him, you will never enlist the lower work of the flesh again. Seeing the gift of God at work and seeing how God uproots the enemy when you place your trust in Him, allows you to see how the enemy, who opposes God's people, operates. He will do his best to keep you relying on the lower-level fleshly strength. He wants to operate in the spirit where he is mostly unseen, while he wants you to operate in the weak flesh. This way he's guaranteed a victory. Once you've been enlightened and have seen the results when you allow God to step in, the veil in front of your eyes is removed. No one can convince you that the spiritual world does not exit, nor do you want to live any other way again.

A shift in your confidence

Faith properly understood simply means to stop trying to achieve something in the spiritual realm using human abilities. Human achievement is completely locked out of the spiritual realm; it's not allowed by God. Faith is a total surrender of all human abilities and a complete adoption of God's Word and will. Faith is a gift from God to allow believers to obtain results beyond human abilities. For instance, only by faith can a person be justified in God's eyes for the total removal of sin; by faith science is overturned when Peter walked on water; by faith sickness is healed; by faith the dead are raised; by faith nature bows down to a higher power; by faith God provides where there's nothing; by faith the enemy's forces are overrun by God's authority in a believer's life; by faith, what looks like defeat can be turned around into glorious victory.

The simplicity of faith is expressed in the Apostle Paul's statement to the Philippian church when he said: I am confident that God who began a good work in the believers will carry it on to completion (Philippians 1:6). Chained in jail for the Gospel, Paul wrote this when his life was about to end. The Philippian church was suffering, persecuted and harassed, and the members were experiencing disunity. While in prison, Paul was personally unable to do anything for the church; He trusted God for everything that both they and he needed. Paul's faith was mature enough to do this, but the Philippian church had to grow in their own faith in God. Their suffering and persecution gives us a clear understanding why Paul gave them faith instructions in Philippians 4:6-7. He wanted to anchor their faith in Christ, as his was.

Paul encouraged them to do what he did – to develop the same faith and trust in God as he had amid his suffering and persecution. Paul wanted to give them hope and encourage them not to give up their faith, but to stand firm and place all their hope and anxiety at God's feet in the midst of their extreme difficulties.

Paul encouraged them to emulate his confidence in Christ and he told them that in the past, his confidence had been in his own education, abilities and connections with people in high places. His confidence was in the natural realm and not in Christ. After his encounter with Jesus on the road to Damascus and now being in chains, Paul's life was a demonstration of a shift which had taken place. He had lost confidence in his own abilities and His hope was in Christ. He had the same hope that Jesus would deliver the Philippian church and provide everything they needed. He wanted them to see that a confidence in Christ was the pivotal principle in their suffering; this confidence would deliver anything they might need. He wanted them to hold onto this confidence no matter how unbearable their situation.

From being confident in human abilities to completely relying on God isn't an instantaneous shift; it comes with a gradual understanding in times of suffering. It is a revelation that's needed as the flesh and all its abilities are drained of all boasting and claims. Only through this process can a believer's confidence in themselves shift to a confidence in Christ.

It's not possible for any person to make this shift without undergoing an inner spiritual change during a time of suffering. It takes a total denial of self, a complete surrender, likened to death on a spiritual cross, which gives birth to a total reliance on Christ (Matthew 16:24). The believer must follow the same spiritual path that Jesus followed to the cross for the new person to be resurrected. Jesus is the One Who both initiates and completes this shift (Philippians 1:6).

Hebrews 4 also explains the shift we need in our confidence. Here our weakness and the useless works we do are dealt with and verse 10 makes it clear that a shift from the confidence we place in our own efforts towards a confidence in Jesus our High Priest needs to take place.

Any hope in ourselves will be futile during severe testing, but a hope in Jesus will enable us to remain standing (Hebrews 4:14-16). This is true because Jesus passed the tests and battles so that we can emulate His success by placing our confidence in Him. Through Jesus we have a confidence to approach the throne of God with our problems and needs. This confidence is in the completed work of Jesus Christ.

Chapter 30

The reward of faith

Here are discussion points to describe some of the rewards a believer will experience when walking by faith.

Up to now this book has discussed how the two words of faith and trust are used interchangeably. They both describe a position whereby someone accepts their own inability to help themselves and they reach out to a saviour or a type of Messiah for help.

Jesus made the statement to doubting Thomas that faith will be rewarded by blessings (John 20:29). In this instance Jesus was saying that faith is putting your hope and trust in someone you cannot see, as compared to Him standing in their midst in His resurrected body.

The expression to be "blessed" means to be empowered supernaturally to prosper in the natural. This is something God does for the person who puts their trust in Him. Hebrews 11:6 makes the same statement that anyone who puts their trust in God will be rewarded. By placing your trust in God, you dispose of all other avenues of possible help and you make yourself entirely dependent on God. This is the first part of the Ten Commandments God gave to Israel, stating that they shall have no other gods (Exodus 20:3). To Abraham, the father of our faith and of the nation of Israel, God stepped in as his provider (Genesis 22:14). When you place your trust in someone, the result is that a very intimate relationship develops. Dialogue and an exchange of tangible and intangible things takes place within this relationship. When God supplies a person's needs, for instance, by providing them with daily food as He did with Israel, the person responds by giving thanks and glory to God.

When Jesus made the statement that the believer's faith will be blessed, did Jesus say the reward will be in this world only? Well, when we read the Hebrews 11 accounts of people's lives who put their trust in God, we see something interesting. The people mentioned put their faith or trust in God for things they needed and to obey the call of God to go places and accomplish specific tasks. However, the chapter also highlights an important fact – that the people who placed their trust in God were awaiting their rewards in the life to come. They persisted and endured without wavering until they passed on to the next life where they would receive their eternal rewards.

What we as believers need to meditate on and begin to understand is the whole notion of the next life. While this life is a key indicator of what we will experience in the afterlife, it's not a drop in the ocean compared to the duration of the afterlife. The life we live on earth is the key element in deciding what our next life will look like. Matters such as receiving salvation and the forgiveness of sin, in the present life, is the ultimate indicator of either heaven or hell in the eternal life hereafter (Luke 23:43). In this context, faith is the means that accomplishes this pivotal decision.

Faith is also the mechanism, according to Romans 1:17 and Hebrews 11:6, for the rewards the believer will receive in the next life. Those who walked by faith on earth will be rewarded and Jesus made this clear in John 14:3 when He spoke of the homes He was going to build for those who trust Him. 2 Corinthians 5:10 also speaks of the rewards each believer will receive for their deeds done in the flesh – which are those deeds validated by God. Deeds that warrant a reward can only be those that fall into the category of Hebrews 11:6. Trusting God brings blessings in this life and the life to come.

Managing emotions

Believers need to be able to manage their emotions. Our feelings can be the source of peaks and troughs in our spiritual development, but feelings are often from an unknown source and are, at best, unreliable. Feelings can send us on a completely wrong path, especially when the source of the information we've received is not true. If we analyse these emotions, we realise that they have very little to do with faith.

Feelings or emotions are like waves at sea, coming and going and changing in an instant. Any believer who walks according to their feelings or emotions is weak, unreliable and unstable.

When a believer walks by faith, their feelings or emotions are eliminated. Faith is a gift from the Spirit and it is based on the eternal, inerrant Word of God. Being rooted in God's Word then, ensures that there are no peaks and troughs. The reliability of God's Word brings a stability int the believer's emotions. The more a believer reads and studies Scripture, the more their faith is strengthened. Their emotions are brought under control in a step-by-step process as they put their focus more on God and less on the need or the problem facing them. The effect is that more reliable knowledge allows for deeper trust and deeper trust creates an unshakeable conviction of who Jesus is and why He can be trusted.

When we read Hebrews 11 and Philippians 1:7 we are told how many believers, including Paul, suffered. All but one of the apostles were martyred. Every person who walked their spiritual road by faith will receive their blessings, not in this life but the life to come. Although our trust in and obedience to God are sometimes rewarded in this life, our true reward will be in the life to come. Our eternal rewards will completely outweigh any reward in this present life, which is the theme in Hebrews 11. Earthly possessions can be stolen, deteriorate and decay, while eternal rewards, as Jesus promised in Matthew 6:19-21, cannot.

Suffering in this world

A last important issue regarding the reward of faith is the matter of suffering in this world. This is a weighty issue that has come up in many discussions with both believers and unbelievers. Many people keep a distance from Christianity because of this specific point. When suffering befalls someone, it's not uncommon for both believers and unbelievers to become upset with God. While it is not the author's intent to exhaustively deal with the issue of suffering, if not addressed, outsiders, who are looking into Christianity, will remain confused and sceptical.

The issue of suffering is mentioned in Scripture when faith is discussed. This is because it plays a crucial role in the process of faith – both physically and mentally. Living by faith has the same outworking as the experiences of a believer during a period of fasting. In both instances, the person who lives by faith and the person fasting will undergo developmental pressure. This pressure relates to difficulties experienced both mentally and physically.

True faith strips the person from their own wisdom, resources, strength and abilities. The Bible expresses true faith as a burial of the old person (Galatians 2:20). It's vital step that every believer must undergo. Those who refuse this step, signified by the rite of water baptism after salvation, will find their fallen fleshly egos rise time and time again. When faced with deciding between their own and Godly wisdom, those who have not embraced water baptism and its true meaning, will experience an internal war between the old and new natures within them. The believer must lay down his life and everything that comes with it before he will be able to allow God to take control of his life. Allowing God control is to invite hardships, suffering and opposition. Jesus Himself was said to endure the cross and since He saw the joyful reward ahead in the next life (Hebrews 12:2). Jesus' example informs us that suffering, hardships and unfair treatment for His sake in this life must not be seen as punishment or failure. Although suffering is metaphysically unpleasant and short-lived, its benefits are eternal and irreversible. Suffering form part of the "all things" that work for the good for those who love God and are called according to His purpose (Romans 8:28).

Throughout history, many people have asked why God allows suffering and hardship. Is He distant and disconnected from people's suffering, does He really care, is He insensitive or indifferent? We see it every day when men, women and children suffer around the world. Many ugly things are done to people without God intervening in world He created. To many people, God seems distant and uninterested in humanity's pain. People want to know if God is unable or unwilling to assist?

The answer is in Scripture when we read about an impending reconciliation that will take place, mentioned in Matthew 25:14-30, 2 Corinthians 5:10, Revelation 11:18, Revelation 20:11-15. These passages all speak of an event that will take place in future when the earth as we presently know it is no more. What has been lost in this world will be regained eternally and what has been taken from someone unjustly, will be taken from the perpetrator eternally.

When we as Christians suffer because of setbacks, illness, persecution and unfair treatment, we can remind ourselves what Jesus said in John 16:33. Here He forewarns us that this world, and the enemy's spirit that's prevalent in this world, is opposing God's people. Jesus also said that despite the hardships we face, we will have peace. How can we have peace when we are oppressed? We can have peace because Jesus said He has overcome this world.

He has overcome it and He will make all things new (Isaiah 65:17; 2 Peter 3:13; Revelation 21:1-3). Faith has an immediate and a future aspect to it. When throwing a rock into a pond, there is an immediate splash, but that is not all. After the initial splash, ripples form that keep travelling outward for some time. Faith is the splash and the effects of faith ripple throughout the believer's life and into their future – both earthly and eternally.

Making all things new includes a reconciliation that will be done of every event that took place in this world. God's judgements, His rewards and punishments will be in accordance with people's obedience to His Word. It's clear then that whatever takes place on earth is not the final outcome for any each person; God will have the last say in everything. Both the giving of rewards and revenge are His.

What we as believers need to focus on is that, like the heroes of faith mentioned in Hebrews 11, faith is the key to eternal life with God in the home He is constructing for us. By true faith, we will receive what we have lost in this world for the sake of following Christ. Seeing injustice and cruelty and being the victims of wrongs committed in this world doesn't mean it's over and justice will not be served. Dictators abuse their own people; monsters commit crimes against humanity; murderers take the lives of the innocent, and in the name of financial profits millions lose their lives. By walking in true faith, we can be rooted and grounded in Christ, who is the door to and the guarantee of eternal life. Only with true faith can any person please God and be sure of His promised rewards. By true faith we will be seated with God in heaven and receive back what we have lost on earth for His name's sake (Matthew 19:28-30).

The enemy's strategy is to inflict enough pain, sorrow and suffering to turn the heart of the believer away from God. This is what the writer of Hebrews warned believers against (Hebrews 6:4-6). The same test came to Job in his great affliction (Job 2:9). In many cases pain, distress and suffering can become so intense that the believer abandons all hope and prefers to die.

God will make everything new

See the account of Jonah under the tree where God allowed Jonah to suffer to the point that he wished to die (Jonah 4:5-8). Only true faith empowers the believer not to lose hope but to look beyond their current difficult situation and focus on the eternal life to come, where everything will be brought to book and made new. The book of Revelation describes what the new heaven and earth will be like. Its description is so fitting when it says that God will wipe every tear from the believer's eye. There will be no more death, mourning or crying or pain. God will make everything new.

Imagine a train's tracks running through a country and when it approaches the next country's border, there's a passport control pause for the travellers. The travellers know that this is not their final destination and they patiently wait to depart from there. The formalities completed, the train continues into the new country, towards their final destination. This is what life on earth is like and when death arrives, it represents a change-over after a momentary pause into the new life and whatever the journey held, the final destination makes it all worthwhile.

There are many references in the Bible relating to the believer's home after this life. Jesus, the apostles and the great cloud of witnesses are all cheering the believer on to run their race till the end. Read John 15:19; Philippians 3:20; 1 John 2:15-17; 1 John 5:19; Hebrews 13:14; James 4:4; 1 Peter 2:1-25 and Revelation 21:3-4 – these are references that give the believer hope that it's worth it all to keep their eyes focused on Jesus. I want to end off the section on the reward of faith with a reference to the story mentioned earlier in the section in chapter 19 called, Why Lord? The aged missionary widower who, after decades of service to the church in a foreign land, arrived in his home country to retire. He had no welcoming party, no crowd to witness his hard work and no family members to clap as he received a medal for good service. As he disembarked from the plane, he felt all alone and wished he had a warm reception. He asked God why his efforts were not acknowledged and why no one arrived to welcome him home. Suddenly, he felt in his heart God saying to him: "But, you are not home yet."

What an encouraging story this is to every believer who has and currently is enduring suffering and difficulties because of their trust in God. What an example to all believers this missionary set. He was able to endure, to fight to the end and not lose focus of the real prize – which Paul describes as "the high calling of God in Christ Jesus". (Philippians 3:14 KJV). Paul understood that his salvation was not the complete plan of God. While the believer's salvation begins in this life, its true culmination is in the life to come. For every believer, this glorious event will either begin with Jesus' second coming or the believer's death. For this reason, Paul says that he has not yet attained the final reward for placing his complete trust in God. The heavenly reward outshines anything else is the end-plan of God regarding the believer's salvation and is guaranteed for everyone who puts their trust in Christ.

If faith is a gift from our Father in heaven, then it is obvious He gave it to us to achieve something special. He didn't give it to us mix it up with worldly wealth. He gave us this amazing gift to help us in our daily tasks and, more importantly, to achieve eternity. Trusting God when the storm seems just too powerful is what it is about; holding onto your faith and letting God. Imagine the eternal joy when you stand before God's throne and He expresses His pleasure for maintaining your faith. Is that not the sweetest eternal reward?

If there is a reward for walking by faith, it is to know Jesus intimately for eternity. Through this process we share in His inheritance and His joy. Putting our faith in Him is to trust Him, to know Him. If this is the case, then the inverse of not trusting Jesus it not to know Him and then to be told to depart from Him (Matthew 7:23).

Chapter 31

Question your resolve

Resolve means to have a firm determination to do something or a definite decision on a course of action. The walk of true faith will bring every believer to a pivotal point where they must decide to either change or hold onto their current resolve. To change a resolve means the believer must go through a deep valley experience – and the believer who emerges from the valley will not be the same person.

Paul mentions his valley in 2 Corinthians 12: 8 where he says he asked God three times to take away his burden, yet God did not take Paul out of the valley.

Hebrews 11 mentions the afflictions that the believers experienced. David speaks about being in a valley of death (Psalm 23:4). He uses the analogy of a valley as a model for us, a new way of thinking to be followed throughout our lives. He depicts his experience as a dark valley and rightfully so, because his life was threatened by King Saul. David uses the image of a dark valley to powerfully illustrate what his test felt like, and the valley he describes shows how people are unable to rescue themselves and their desperate need for the comfort a higher power brings. David's image of the deep valley contrasts with his unwavering faith and confidence in God to guide him through his difficult time.

The experience of a deep valley introduces an important point. At the outset of this book, we saw that faith only works when we're unable to do anything ourselves. Faith is a gift from God; no human can earn salvation in any way. Faith alone is what enables us to receive eternal life (John 3:16 and Ephesians 2:8-9). Faith starts when the believer lets go of all their abilities and resources and looks to God for help – it waits for the end of human pride and boasting. Another expression of faith is: "If it were not for God."

The deep valley describes that moment when the believer has nowhere else to turn for help but to God and it is embodied in Jesus' struggle in the Garden of Gethsemane, leading up to the cross. He had the ability to act in any way He chose, yet, in a total trust in and obedience to His Father, Jesus surrendered His all and expressed His desire for the will of His Father to prevail (Isaiah 53:10). Being weak, vulnerable and suffering, Jesus was under pressure from the enemy to follow His own will, as He was when He underwent temptation when He fasted for forty days (Matthew 4:1-11).

To illustrate the journey of faith and what it entails, I'm sharing this personal account. When I decided to walk by true faith, I experienced several deep valleys and I became convinced that no believer, having walked through a deep valley, could ever be the same.

The reason I mentioned 'resolve' earlier is because it represents the standard that every person sets for themselves and what they use as a guideline in life. A resolve is something a person holds onto, no matter what.

S deep valley experience questions a believer's resolve. It is important that when the believer experiences the valley, they should be attentive and learn as much as they can from the experience. They must be mindful of the test they're in, what it's doing in them and how it challenges their resolve. In this way, they'll be able to approach their next faith challenge in a better way. A deep walk of faith generally tears into our earthly existence like nothing else can. It's worth noting some experiences you've been through so that when the next great faith challenge comes you can be victorious. God is faithful and patient with every believer as they develop into mature Christians.

The process of faith questions a person's resolve; their convictions and beliefs. We need to have our faith resolve challenged, because change cannot come unless what we believe is tested. There is great truth in the tests we undergo. How do we know if the convictions and beliefs we hold to are true, complete and trustworthy, unless they are exposed, examined and validated? We cannot place our trust in something that hasn't been tested. Every believer should know the importance of knowing the Word of God. This is where our resolve should be – in God's infallible, inerrant, eternal, immutable and inspired Word. The best way to develop a sound resolve is to have it tested and then make the necessary changes. I call this the post-completion resolve. If we're willing to undergo tests to examine and cement our resolve, we can face any test with the full confidence that Jesus had.

The Spirit of God wants to assist the believer to turn valleys into hills – tests into victories. Remember, He is the One who led Jesus into the desert to be tempted (Matthew 4:1). He will also lead us into battles. One of the most comforting aspects of this is that He is with us during the battle; He never leaves us to fight on our own. He wants us to reach the realisation that we're unable to fight a spiritual enemy. He wants us to call on Him to step in. He wants us to humble ourselves, acknowledge our weakness and hand our battles over to Him to fight on our behalf.

Trench warfare

Trench warfare is a good illustration of the battle that rages when a believer enters the journey of true faith. This warfare is also called the slow grind or a war of attrition. It's when the enemy tries to wear down its opponent through sustained attack and pressure and it feels like wave after wave of enemy fire raining down on you.

Each day you decide to make it a success, only to be pushed down again by the enemy. When in a trench, you're not able to decide to exit your situation; you have to hunker down, embrace the situation and be ready for inner change. The slow grind description relates to the drawn out aspect of the warfare, progress is slow and you get shot at every time you stick your head out. Trench warfare is a season you commit to for the long run.

In the trenches, you face an enemy you cannot see out in the open, and you must come to terms with long periods spent underground, which can be a very disheartening place. You must learn how manage your thoughts, maintain a healthy frame of mind and stick to a rigorous routine. The trench cuts off dreams of selfish future self-promotion or personal preferences. Following orders is crucial. Standing up and charging the enemy is not an option. You will only get hurt or even killed. This is because the definition of faith says the believer must lay down their own efforts to try to their salvation. Faith requires that the believer invites God's hand into his situation. A soldier in the trenches cannot make a difference to his situation. The most effective approach is when the soldier calls on a higher power to do what he cannot do in his own strength. This is how faith is activated; the person asks God to step into their situation to defeat the enemy. The only thing the believer can be commended for is the fact that they surrendered their will and desire to act and called on the Lord to intervene.

Each season in the trenches prepares you for the next battle and lessons learnt yesterday can be applied today. Each opportunity to fight and resist the enemy is a learning curve and every day you learn to cope with new challenges. What felt unbearable yesterday becomes tomorrow's norm.

Trench warfare requires that a fighter learns to cope with the challenges it brings. A soldier might walk confidently into a trench, but is soon humbled by the enemy's relentless bombard-ments. Weeks and months of pressure by the enemy can give rise to thoughts of desperation and surrender and it's not uncommon for soldiers to lift a white flag and surrender when life in the trenches became unbearable. It is a slow daily grind as the enemy tries to convince the believer to poke their head out of the trench. Each day in the trench teaches you that the end is near and the battle is not without purpose. Understanding the journey and making intentional mental notes will help the believer to grow internally. One battle lost does not mean the war is lost. Those who surrender are the ones who ignorantly make the same mistakes time and time again. First, they're not mindful of the journey and second, they don't learn from their mistakes. Making mental notes prevents the enemy from catching the believer with the same lure each time.

When a believer finds themself in the trenches of a faith challenge, they cannot see the light of day. All they see and hear is the enemy's constant bombardment on their life – from a sudden financial challenge, to rumours of job retrenchments, to a health scare and many more. Every time the believer dares to raise their head out of the trench, they are shot at. Mental notes enable the believer to be better prepared for the next faith challenge. By upskilling themself in the realm of faith warfare, the believer undergoes a transformation whereby they thrive in difficult situations. They no longer see and experience tough faith challenges as obstacles. They view them as development opportunities, using what they've learnt in previous challenges to guide them to victory each time.

Every beautiful sunrise

Passing through a faith valley has an eternal effect on a believer and having walked a path of true faith strips the believer of all rights, claims and boasting. All that remains is for them to lift their hands and proclaim the goodness and greatness of God. There is no boasting in the flesh; the boasting is in what Jesus has done.

The path of true faith takes the believer on a journey where this world and all it offers becomes strangely dim. Nothing it can offer will ever compare to a life lived by faith because faith has nothing in common with the flesh and its boasting.

Having passed through a faith valley, I know another valley will come – guaranteed. The patterns in Scripture are clear regarding this.

The journey of faith causes a profound change in the believer's thinking. It is like a person lying on a surgeon's bed whose heart had stopped and the doctor has called time of death. Death is saying goodbye to every worldly item, it's the end of every plan, desire and dream. Then suddenly the person is revived and within a few days is sent home. From that point on the person lives from moment to moment, fully appreciating every breath they take, every beautiful sunrise and sunset and every chirping bird. Everything is a reminder of the goodness and sovereignty of God. Being on a surgeon's table is one level of trust, but being in God's hands is another level of trust.

Tasting true faith in God is a journey of spiritual warfare, of peace and surrender; it's a journey of great spiritual power, a funeral of the flesh and all it represents. It is a beautiful sunrise – a new day God has made.

Chapter 32

Final remarks

Someone has to say it

Yes, people are frail and fallible in all their ways. Without God they can do nothing. Since the fall of man, they've tried everything to prove their own worth. People have always sought a way to exit without God sustaining them. People will never be able to survive on their own, let alone inherit eternal life without God. Humanity was created by God, and while they carry the breath of God in they, they're subject to God's rule and authority.

One of their greatest hurdles that must be overcome is not to look at God from a human perspective. Trying to understand the creator and sustainer of the universe using the human mind and reasoning, will always fall short.

The Old Testament shows God as the Father of the nation of Israel – the One who led them and fed them. He is also the One who sent poisonous snakes to bite the people who murmured against Him. While God punished the people for their rebellion, He also sent a mechanism to heal those who were bitten (Numbers 21:8-9). God also condemned an entire city, men women and children, because of their pagan practices (Joshua 6:17-19). God's holiness can never be called into question and His nature will never accepts anything that is not holy, no matter how small, and it will never allow people to dictate a situation to Him. God is unchangeable and so are His plans and purposes.

When we walk by faith, it is crucial that we understand what Jesus said in the Gospels. God looks after our needs, not our wants (Matthew 6:27-34). When we put Him first and submit to His all-knowing wisdom, we can be sure our lives are in His hands. This is truly a great comfort and an eternal assurance because there's nothing and no one else who's always the same and is always faithful. God alone is worthy to be trusted. He is the ever-present God who loves us and wants the best for us. He is not just committed to every believer – He is totally involved in the life of every believer.

God is in all, He's above all, He's all-knowing, all-seeing and all-powerful. His ways are higher than our ways and He's in the process of rolling out an eternal plan that includes every individual.

In many instances when we put our trust in God for something specific, we end up learning a good lesson when the answer or fulfilment tarries. Or something we expect God to do for us might be against His will for our lives and in opposition to His great plan. In such a case, although we approach God with great expectation, we need to always remember He is the all-knowing God who decides everything.

1 Corinthians 13:9-12 says that a time will soon come when we will know as we have been known. We will understand with a new mind why God made the decisions He made. For now, we must be honest and say that we don't know everything.

> For we know in part and we prophesy in part, but when completeness comes, what is in part disappears. 1 Corinthians 9:10,11 (NIV)

We don't have the mind of God and at best, with deep insight and continued studying Scripture, we're able to a see a glimpse of God's ways. The best way to approach God is given to us in Hebrews 11:6. Here the author explains that anyone who comes to God must believe that He exists and that He rewards those who seek Him. In plain terms, to seek after a power greater than yourself requires submission, reverence and respect. It paints the picture of a benefactor and a beneficiary. God is our benefactor and we are the recipients of His love. We are to submit to His will and His ways to truly benefit from His kindness. It's here where many believers get it wrong. When "walking by faith". they approach God with a sense of arrogance and not the reverent respect He is due. They place their needs and wants at His feet and blindly expect the benefactor to fulfil their requests.

When looking at God from a human perspective, people easily get angry and confused and they lose hope. We must always remember that He's the potter and we're the clay. We're in no position to demand things from Him, nor should we abuse the gifts He has given us and use them in a way that dishonours Him. Our attitude should like Job's:

Though he slay me, yet will I hope in him; Job
13:15 (**NIV**)

Abraham also argued that God was able to raise Isaac from the
dead. He knew if he obeyed God's will, his future would be taken
care of and the promise to his children's children would be
fulfilled. He understood that the One who created and named
every star in the sky can do the impossible.

As Jesus said, His Father works in this life and the life to come. We
often forget how God sees time. He exists, acts and functions
within a space and time that doesn't correlate with ours as
humans. As believers, we view success as the fulfilment of a
request while we're here on earth. But we read the accounts of
believers who trusted God in this life and only received the fulfilment of their rewards in the life to come (Hebrews 11:12-18).
This tells us that God operates in a dimension that incorporates
this time on earth and beyond it.

The believers in Hebrews 11 acted on God's promises while still
alive but were rewarded in the life after death. We can imagine
how they waited for the promises of God while on earth but had
to surrender their spirits into God's hands when they died. Yet
they did not lose heart. They held onto God's promises, knowing
He cannot lie and that they'll receive what God promised. If they
received what they were promised while on earth, the plan of
God would have had to shrink to fit into human expectations.
This is proof that God is the God of all and over all. He has in
His hands the keys to life and death. God is the rewarder of those
who diligently seek Him and He can reward them in this life and
or the one to come.

When we read the accounts of how God dealt with His own people, not allowing a single sin to go unpunished, we begin to understand that God will deal with us in the same manner. When Jesus says judgement will begin with His own house, how dreadful it will be when He judges those who ignored His gift of salvation by grace through faith. In the account of Noah, no person on earth who remained outside the ark was spared. When Moses instructed the Israelites to put the blood of the lamb on their doorposts, no firstborn was spared in those houses that had no blood on the doorposts. A time will come when every person who ignored God's gracious gift of His Son will experience His eternal judgement. Since the beginning of time, God remains unchangeable and the only way to Him is by faith.

About the Author

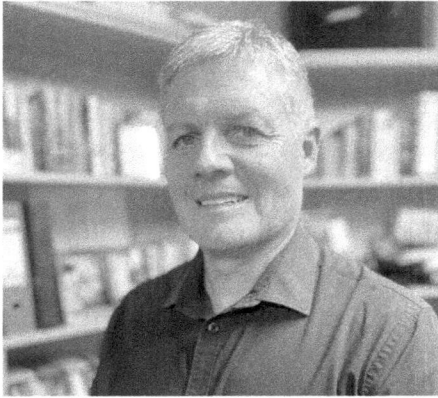

The author has been serving as a pastor in various pastoral roles since the age of eighteen and is currently serving in the Pentecostal Holiness Church in Phokeng, near the town of Rustenburg in the North-West Province, South Africa. The author has been involved in producing educational material for discipleship training programs and courses to train aspiring preachers and teachers in the local church. The denominational church affiliation the author is currently serving in, has its roots in the 1909 Azusa Street Revival in the USA. The current church in its African setting has a global reach into many countries and continents.

The author is trained as a chartered accountant and holds a post-graduate degree in Theology. He has extensive experience in both the corporate world and church missions. Having travelled extensively, the author has a fair understanding of diverse cultures in and outside the church. He has also studied how other religions stand up to the true Gospel of Christ. Part of the author's research and passion is to understand the Theological basis and practical outworking of the relationship between God and mankind. Over many years the author has devoted time and energy to help believers in the church to know God better. It is the author's resolve to see believers invest their time, energy and talents in what is of eternal worth, compared to temporary worldly happiness. It is the author's deep conviction that God has something amazing in store for every believer, which goes much further than just being saved from their sin. The author's work will draw the believer's attention to God's true intention regarding their salvation.

It has been the author's personal journey to seek and understand why God wants to reconcile people to Himself. As a person actively involved in managing a family business, the author has seen and experienced both the lure and the deceitfulness of worldly wealth. The author has seen God involve Himself in his personal life, causing him to ask: Is there perhaps something more to the average Christian life we are missing out on?

www.ingramcontent.com/pod-product-compliance
Lightning Source LLC
Chambersburg PA
CBHW061818040426
42447CB00012B/2711